Dear April,

What an experience it was to have you participate and contribute to Reimagine the in Stoos in July 2019. Do not forget all the cowbells :·

Thomas

4th of July '19
Stoos, CH

Dear April,

Thank you for your openness and partnership. I look forward to discovering where our paths will continue to cross.

Jul

"Find Your Horizon"

....

PRAISE FOR LIVE
WITH INTENT

"Having worked with Justin and Thomas during the 1990s, I know that they are two mavericks with big, bold ideas. Their talent is to go deep inside companies and add serious value. If you seek to discover who you are and where you want to go, and if you desire to develop personal and team effectiveness, I recommend you dive deep into this book. Be bold; question the unexamined assumptions in your life; and emerge a more powerful you!"

~**Stephen M. R. Covey**, *The New York Times bestselling author of The Speed of Trust and coauthor of Smart Trust*

"What we need in this ever-changing, more competitive global environment is a better understanding of our personal abilities and our human potential. This book will guide your journey towards extraordinary achievement."

~**Nido R. Qubein**, *President, High Point University*

"Like Reichart and Tomlinson, I see self-leadership as a creative activity. This book will help you in your quest to become a true leader, worthy of emulation."

~**Eileen McDargh**, *www.trueleadercreed.com and www.theresiliencygroup.com*

"You are the author of your life story, so why not make it a Love Story? You will love life, love others and love yourself even more by reading and applying the advice in *Live with Intent*. More than that, you will change the world."

~**Lance Secretan**, *advisor to leaders and author of Love Story*

"Having helped hundreds of small business owners to start and grow their companies, I can attest that Reichart and Tomlinson are right: being creative, proactive, positive and resourceful enables you to achieve and sustain success. The simple structure... where are you now, where do you want to go, and what do you need to do to get there... makes this book a must-read."

~**Eric Thompson**, *Vice President, SCORE SE Region*

"Reading through the first pages of this incredible book opened my eyes to concepts I hadn't considered, such as the seasons, the matter, the direction, the place I'm in now and where I want to go in the creation of my life. I broke all the rules—read through the entire book as quickly as possible to consume the information, and my mind has expanded exponentially. Now I'm going back to apply the principles. I see this book as a manual for creating my ultimate life—thank you Thomas and Justin for being guides in shaping my future! Everybody needs this book!"

~**Jason Hewlett**, *CSP, CPAE Speaker Hall of Fame, author, award-winning entertainer*

"You're holding a book that will not only expand your thinking—but also transform your life and grow your business. Written for people who want to define what really matters. Written by the two greatest business thinkers on the rationale of how human capital can create, plan and deliver value in organizations."

~**Henrik von Scheel**, *Co-founder of LEADing Practice, Board Member @ Google EMEA, Gazprom, Global University Alliance, World Economic Forum & UN*

"In a world of increasing learned helplessness, *Live with Intent* is a much needed practical, step-by-step guide to take charge and make your success happen. Everyone knows you need to find what you love, to follow your passion, in order to find success. But no one tells you how. Finally, with a masterful stroke of clarity and genius, Thomas and Justin have done it."

~**Jake Herway**, *Organizational Effectiveness Subject Matter Expert, Gallup*

"If you think you've had your fill of self-help books, think again. This book is unique—something to be savored. The authors offer philosophy and provide all the steps you need to take charge of your career and life. Their questions, insights, and tips are timeless and timely. Keep this book handy, so you can dog-ear the pages and circle sentences that are most meaningful to you (as I did)! The authors take you on a journey. Because they pull good, bad and ugly lessons from their own lives, you feel like they are personally talking to you. They become your personal coaches at every step of the journey you are about to take. What a lovely gift!"

~**Beverly Kaye**, *founder, Career Systems International, and coauthor of Help Them Grow or Watch Them Go: Career Conversations Employees Want and Love 'Em Or Lose 'Em: Getting Good People to Stay*

"Congrats to the authors on a fine, engrossing book. Ken Shelton delivers a powerful foreword, as is his way, and the authors deliver on their far-reaching book promise—to get you where you want to go in life. In my three decades in corporate leadership development, I've witnessed first-hand both the best and worst of leadership. As Reichart and Tomlinson teach in this book, how we lead ourselves influences how we lead others: We can't separate personal and professional."

~**Michael Winston**, *author of World-Class Performance*

"Having served four U.S. Presidents and numerous international commerce entities, in numerous assignments around the world, I have seen firsthand the value of helping people develop principle-centered lives. Until now, the remarkable work of Thomas and Justin has been limited to those who have had the privilege of working directly with them. I am pleased to see that through *Live with Intent*, anyone can now access their insights for living more purposeful and productive lives. How I wish that individual contributors, institutions, and commerce around the world would embrace and live these principles—that would make all the difference. It would make our world more stable, more reliable in bringing people and purpose into the center of all of our lives. "

~**Ambassador Gregory John Newell**, *Former Ambassador to Sweden of the United States of America, former U.S. Assistant Secretary of State for International Organization Affairs, Special Assistant in the White House to the President and Director of Presidential Appointments*

"This book is a refreshing reminder to be bold and to live passionately! It's as widely relevant as the wisdom it contains. Each chapter outlines an important step on our journey to transform old habits into better ones. Justin and Thomas guide us in living with intent by making timely applications of their timeless principles of leadership."

~**Mustapha El Akkari**, *Global Supply Management, NuSkin Enterprises*

"As a pattern specialist, I work with identifying issues and trying to identify repeatable patterns to create a better future. I was delighted when asked to be involved in this wonderful piece of work. It offers successful patterns of understanding where you are. It helps define, imagine and design where you are trying to go, as well as offering practical guidelines and methods of how you can get there. I'm proud to know and have worked with the authors directly and invite anybody holding this book to start your journey of creating your future."

~Prof. Mark von Rosing, *Global University Alliance Chairman, ISO Development Member, NATO Sr. Advisor, United Nations Strategic Advisor*

"In order to create a life of meaning and impact resonant with the volatile and uncertain times in which we live, leaders must embark on an earnest journey of self-insight and self-awareness. Thomas and Justin have expertly and elegantly uncovered universal, human principles that help make this endeavor not only real, but also enthralling. With specific exercises and clear guidelines, the authors offer a rich path to personal mastery, fulfillment, resilience and leadership. This book contains much-needed wisdom for those who embrace growth at any age."

~Michael Chavez, *CEO Duke Corporate Education*

"We live in a world that is "demanding by design". It changes at a very fast pace and as leaders, we can not take advantage of new opportunities or resolve existing challenges based on the current way of thinking. *Live with Intent* portraits 12 principles that will serve as the foundation for a transformational journey. This book will become a reference for anyone who would like to leave a mark in his/her life, being at a personal and/or professional level. I have worked with both authors at different times in my career and have had the privilege to see real time, how the principles described in this book transform people's lives. So yes, change, fulfilment and success are all possible. By reading this book you have a wonderful chance to expand your horizons and to live with intent."

~**Alvaro Soto**, *Sub Regional Head*
LATAM - Roche Pharmaceuticals

"This is an engaging book, full of distilled wisdom, presented in a warm and personal manner. Every reader will find a nugget that will elevate their life."

~**Jack Zenger**, *CEO of Zenger Folkman, best-selling*
author of Speed: How Leaders Accelerate Successful Execution

"Justin and Thomas have created trusting and fun-loving relationships in their work and their lives. They have lived in and done business in many countries around the world, allowing them to gain a broader and more diverse perspective of different cultures and work environments. Justin and Thomas were able to create this book because they practice the principles related to living their lives intentionally. When we see ourselves a part of a living system instead of being apart from it, we begin to see the importance of learning and living with natural laws and principles that surround us. *Live with Intent* provides a unique approach to thinking about the principles that allow us to grow and evolve in an ever-changing world."

~**Tom James**, *CEO Vansing Distribution Group*
and author of Tea on the Serengeti: Finding our
Natural Rhythm in an ever-changing world

"I loved what I read. The principles are not over-wrought. They are simple and ring true and are illustrated with personal and professional cases that are inspiring, uplifting and often painful. I'd pay for a copy just to read the stories and anecdotes that illustrate the principles."

~**Dow Wilson**, *CEO Varian Medical Systems*

"*Live with Intent* offers a simple framework for being agile in a complex and global environment."

~**Dr. Alan Hippe**, *F. Hoffmann–La Roche Ltd,*
Chief Financial Officer and Member of the
Corporate Executive Committee

"We do not need ideas, tolls and hints of yesterday. What we need in this tsunami of global change is that we discover, understand and accept ourselves. That's why this book is a tool for discovering and a way of understanding yourself and a true hope for you. So: sell all your HOW TO XY books and buy this one. The surprise and the success will be yours. "

~**Peter Seibt**, *#1 bestseller, The New*
Nomads and All 7 Tools of Change

"In their new book *Live with Intent,* Thomas Reichart and Justin Tomlinson bring together vital elements into a clear, workable step by step plan for the reader to consciously create their own successful life and career with an authenticity that's truly meaningful. I will be referring to their book as I take my next steps into my own future. I recommend you do the same!"

~**Marilyn McLeod**, *Author, Speaker, Executive Coach*

"The book's structure and easy-to-follow concepts and illustrations provide the reader with the necessary tool and mindset to lead a more happy, successful and meaningful life, both in private and business. Gift it to yourself. Reading and following its advice and insight might well be the greatest present you can give to yourself, your family, friends and business associates."

~**Thomas Kummer-Hardt**, *Media Executive & International Business-IT Consultant*

"Reading this book was VERY exciting. This is indeed not yet another book on development; it is special. It offers an enjoyable and constructive journey, where the reader is guided step by step to follow tips, develop personal frameworks, leverage powerful unexploited inner abilities and strength so as to become the architect of his/her future: this comprehensive approach is powerful. Justin and Thomas' perspectives and stories provide additional and personal perspectives, which make that journey feel easy. I particularly enjoyed the starting assumption that we all are gifted and have a lot to contribute: to our self, our relatives, friends, and colleagues and we owe it to all of them to make sure we make a positive difference. Working with the aim to build a constructive legacy is definitely very motivating! Thank you both for this great book."

~**Boris L. Zaïtra**, *Global Head of Mergers & Acquisitions F. Hoffmann-La Roche Ltd.*

"The value of a great book is found in the ability to apply what you learn, and *Live with Intent* is a great book! Justin and Thomas offer you a practical guide for applying principles of personal effectiveness. You will find yourself blessed in important, positive ways. This book will expand your capacity to live a life that matters."

~**Ron McMillan,** *4x New York Times bestselling author and co-author of Crucial Conversations*

Made For Success Publishing
P.O. Box 1775 Issaquah, WA 98027
www.MadeForSuccessPublishing.com

Distributed by Made For Success Publishing
Copy Editor Anja Hemming-Xavier, WeSwitch Languages
GmbH & Co. KG, Germany

Library of Congress Cataloging-in-Publication data
Reichart, Thomas
Tomlinson, Justin
    Live with Intent: Creating Your Future
       p. cm.

       ISBN: 9781613398975
       LCCN: 2017905983

LIVE WITH INTENT

CREATING YOUR FUTURE

....

THOMAS REICHART

JUSTIN TOMLINSON

....

DEDICATION

To the late Stephen R. Covey—thank you for your life and the immense contribution you are still making to humanity. It was a pleasure working with and learning from you.

To Friedrich von Rohrscheidt—thank you for the long walks along the runway in Bavaria, South Germany and for all the conversations they inspired.

To Peter Seibt—thank you for inspiring us toward new horizons; they are giving us the courage to live life on our own terms.

CONTENTS

FOREWORD

....

Ken Shelton is the recipient of the 2015 Global Leadership Excellence Award from the World Leadership Council and has been editor/publisher of Leadership Excellence magazine for 30 years.

"Who Are These Guys?

And why should you listen to them?"

Do you remember the scene in the movie "Butch Cassidy and the Sundance Kid," starring Paul Newman and Robert Redford, when the two outlaws wonder aloud, after failing to lose the expert Native-American-led party tracking them: "Who are these guys?"

I'm pleased that two of my expert friends on performance and transformation, Thomas Reichart and Justin Tomlinson, natives of Germany and America, invited me to write a Foreword for this meaningful book. While you are reading it, you might also wonder: "Who are these guys?" They are experts at getting you from where you are now to where you want to go in life and business. They have proven their expertise as organizational and leadership consultants and executive coaches around the world.

About Reichart: I recall with fondness my initial meeting with Thomas when he was working at Rentrop publishing in Germany. Young at the time, he was already serving as a profit center manager and special appointee of the CEO. We had agreed to meet at his office in Bonn-Bad Godesberg. I expressed concern about navigating my way from the airport to the train station and then to his office, so I asked him to pick me up or arrange a transport service.

Thinking that I had requested VIP treatment, he arranged for a limo to meet me at the train station. Meanwhile, I never got the message and took a bus into the city.

At a central plaza, I called him. He asked me three questions:

Where are you now?

Where are you trying to go?

How can we get you there?

After subsequent meetings with Thomas in New York and Utah, I made a second trip to Frankfurt. I had flown into Zurich and then boarded a train from Zurich to Munich, where he had met me. I then rode with him in his BMW to Frankfurt, as we discussed his career path.

I asked him three questions:

Where are you now?

Where are you trying to go?

How can we get you there?

On the same trip I somewhat reluctantly agreed to be a passenger on a small airplane—with Thomas serving as a pilot—and fly along the Rhine River. I enjoyed the ride until the turbulence increased with an approaching storm.

Later, I hopped on a bicycle and rode with him on narrow, winding paths through a forest near his home. We then biked for another hour just to buy bread, sausages, and butter for a remarkable Saturday breakfast. He pedaled fast, and I struggled to keep up with him.

Both in the airplane and on the bike, I asked him:

Where are we now?

Where are we trying to go?

How can we get safely there?

How do these memories and questions relate to this book? These same three questions constitute the core structure of this book—a book that I discussed with him in some detail two decades ago when he was relatively young before much of life's opposition had hit him hard. Frankly, I've been amazed at his resilience. Thomas is an action figure, always moving; a pathfinder, always trailblazing; a pilot, always flying high with high hopes (and little sleep). He seems born for adventure and adversity. Thomas has managed to run large enterprises over a decade while simultaneously meeting the high demands of a series of medical crises involving his three children; that he has been able to do this is truly extraordinary. But I am also impressed with his passion for learning and human transformation, which has led him to extract timeless principles that he is now sharing in this book. In light of all these experiences, I consider him to be a very credible author.

About Tomlinson: I first met Justin Tomlinson in 1993 at the Covey Leadership Center. He was part of the marketing team for *Executive Excellence*, a magazine published at that time by me, in partnership with the Covey Leadership Center in the USA. After a series of entrepreneurial product launches for Covey, Justin was given the opportunity to start up a new organization in Continental Europe for the newly merged FranklinCovey company.

Justin has a unique life philosophy where the fun is woven into his operative life. Rarely does a week go by without some type of adventure—boating, rafting, motorcycling, biking, or back-country skiing. Somehow he finds a way to blend adventure with his work constantly. A typical month includes: discovering a new country somewhere in the world; spending a weekend in his mountain home in the Swiss Alps; and making it home to the USA for a river run with his family after business meetings in Basel, Munich, Istanbul and San Francisco. His neighbors at home are convinced he is a spy as this is the only explanation for his nomadic life!

Luckily for Justin, he met Thomas shortly after moving to Belgium in 1998. Thomas became his personal guide for all things pertaining to working and living in Europe. Instant friends, they have coached each other through the highs and lows of life. What was intended as a three-year European assignment with FranklinCovey has turned into an 18-year friendship and European adventure with Thomas that still continues today. This book, *Live with Intent*, is the product of their experiences together and on their own. Personal and business setbacks have been no match for their resilience.

Together, Thomas and Justin are a rare team—a strong consulting team that personifies true synergy, where the whole is exponentially greater than the sum of its parts. Clients who work with them say: "Together they are magic." They possess an amazing ability to solve difficult problems and inspire people in their work and personal lives.

Live with Intent is evidence of how we can indeed create ourselves and thereby create our future. We can live life on our own terms. Thomas and Justin—and their book—can help get you where you want to go. So buckle up for the ride of your life and be prepared to grow as you seek and explore new horizons in your life.

....

YOUR CREATIVE CAPACITY

"BE A LEADER, AND ENJOY AN INTENTIONAL LIFE."

Your ability to lead effectively depends on the wise and intentional deployment of your creative capacity—your skillset and mindset, your education and experience, your flexibility and adaptability, your local and global perspectives, your innovation and execution.

Thomas: I have experienced many wonderful things in my life. My family and my colleagues have sometimes said that we should make a movie out of the exciting and unbelievable things that have happened to me. Indeed, I often asked myself: Why is my life almost as exciting and breathtaking as many great movies and thrillers on television and in the cinemas?

I think it is due to the enormous dynamics of some situations and to my incurable curiosity of meeting interesting people to create something meaningful together.

Some people have said that I've had a "charmed life," that I was born on "the sunny side" of life, forever being there.

Yes, I feel highly blessed by life, even with all the ups and downs that have happened to me. In this book, I share many of these vicissitudes—like surviving multiple life-threatening plane incidents as a pilot of WWII warbirds and as a pilot of modern planes; raising three children, all of whom faced life-threatening health challenges before they were five years old; and building and selling the first online grocery store in Germany just as the global IT bubble burst.

What I have learned is this: We can create our lives and build our careers, our businesses, for better and for worse, with our intentions—our will and plan to turn our hopes, dreams, aspirations, and visions into reality.

I think this notion is very exciting, because life is a wonderful and endlessly precious gift, even with all the ascending and descending currents. As an aircraft pilot, I can appreciate the difference between favorable conditions and extreme challenges.

I, for one, am forever grateful that we are allowed to make our own choices—that we are allowed to create ourselves—as long as we retain our basic human rights and remain free from controlling addictions and conditions.

The "how" of this self-creation (or re-creation) has fascinated me for over 25 years in my work as a business consultant. In a sense, this book is my answer to one of the most critical questions in life: How can I create a life (and business) that is meaningful to me, defined by my own values, and determined by my own choices?

I approach this book with this question in mind. And my hope is that this book will enable you to create a more meaningful life and thriving business.

What will be the result? What will be your personal return on investment? Think of people you have met in life who you would say are really exceptional and inspiring to you. As you consider these people, I presume you have come across some of these character traits: giving freely; serving others; team-player; are present; are helpful, etc.

We like to remember people we have met with true grandeur. People with remarkable character and goodness, mostly since they have influenced our lives for the positive. We like being in their presence. We all should strive to become examples of true grandeur. We could say:

True grandeur is full of patience.

True grandeur is giving.

True grandeur will not look at one's own advantage only.

True grandeur means staying patient in all circumstances.

True grandeur is not easy to be enticed by greed.

True grandeur means forgiving.

True grandeur does not find fault.

Please ask yourself if you agree the three main value killers are:
1. Anger
2. Greed
3. Pride

Imagine how grand your personal and professional life could be with more patience, giving and forgiving. It is worth the effort to strive for such grandeur in the way we love, lead and teach by precept and by example.

Justin: In fall 1981, I was about to leave my home to enjoy a fun, well-planned day with my friends. As the door was closing behind me, my mother reminded me of a commitment I had accepted weeks before—a service project for Mrs. Winters, a widow living in our neighborhood.

I thought to myself: Why can't mothers mind their own business!? There are plenty of other boys for the service project. They don't need me. I decided not to go.

When I informed my mother that I wasn't going, a small war broke out in my home—and I lost the battle.

Thirty minutes later I arrived at Mrs. Winters' home—defeated and determined to punish my mother by making it a miserable day for everyone.

My anger was channeled into an irrigation ditch, where I was assigned to clear the overgrown grass and leaves. The work was hard and required hours of digging.

At first, I resented being assigned the difficult and dirty chore of ditch-digging, but somehow the anger gradually left me as I began taking satisfaction in the perfectly shaped ditch emerging from my work.

But that was just the start of the transformation. I could see how our work was impacting everyone involved. First of all, the yard went from complete disarray to a well-landscaped yard. With the help of many small hands the leaves, the ditches, the woodpile and the grass were taken care of. And then I could see the other boys involved actually appeared to be having fun. They were laughing and teasing each other as they worked. In reality, I was having fun, too. Perhaps a different kind of fun than playing sports, hanging out with friends or going to a movie. This type of fun filled me with a sense of joy and happiness. The heaviness I felt when I arrived and resisted was gone. Life somehow did feel lighter, easier and connected to something bigger than myself. It was like being involved in something important.

I look back on that day as my earliest memory of consciously creating my life—a life of recreating the happiness I saw mirrored on Mrs. Winters' face. I have since verified that doing meaningful work that makes a difference is beyond fun.

Today, I enjoy both the fun that comes from recreation and the fun that comes from service. The best scenario is recreation that involves a deeper purpose. Perhaps our favorite investment is in The Entrepreneur's Academy, a think-tank forum where entrepreneurs come together for an outdoor adventure. The purpose of the adventure is to have fun while helping each other grow our businesses and the meaning we feel in life.

That day in my childhood also marked my first step toward unconsciously creating my profession, my livelihood—adding value by digging "irrigation ditches" to supply water (life-sustaining and growth-producing wisdom in the form of timeless principles) to the world's gardens and farms, companies and factories—in winter, spring, summer, and fall.

Thomas: This is not just another book that you read—you can live it daily! As you internalize these principles, you will experience a very personal and lasting change that will accompany you in your daily routines and forge a secure foundation for the future. In fact, you may look back at some point in life at this moment and think: "This is where it all began."

Every day we are grateful that we had the immense good fortune and privilege to learn the principles we share in the book early in life. Having learned this early is a gift of inestimable value that we do not take for granted.

Our promise to you is this: By learning and applying these 12 universal principles, you will create a life (and business) that is meaningful to you, defined by your own values, and determined by your own choices.

Introduction

INTRODUCTION

....

We often see ourselves in terms of our nationality, title, profession, wealth, religion or the various roles we fill. However, another way to see ourselves is by the value we create for and with other people—our Value-Add or our signature contribution.

Continuously creating a life of meaningful contributions follows a repeatable, natural pattern of knowing where you are now, where you are going, and how you will get there. The simple fact of life is this: Your life (and business) only grows to the extent that you grow.

WHERE YOU ARE NOW

The idea of having different seasons in our lives is familiar to all of us. We often talk about going through different seasons or cycles in life. The four seasons evident in nature are winter, spring, summer, and fall. Many cultures around the world are built around this annual cycle. "Spring break" and "Summer vacation" are examples of how our lives revolve around these seasons. Within this cycle are natural principles that apply to our growth.

What season of life are you in now? How much are you growing each year? In climates where each of the seasons is pronounced, it is easy to see interesting correlations between nature and our own growth patterns. For this reason, we have linked the four seasons to the feeling and desired result of the first four principles of *Live with Intent*.

In Part 1, you examine where you are now in terms of this natural cycle.

Principle	Season	Feeling	Desired Result
Trust	Winter	Turning inside	Build reserves
Freedom	Spring	Blossoming	Make unique contributions
Gratitude	Summer	Slowing down	Be in the present
Self-Confidence	Autumn	Letting go	Reap the harvest

WHERE YOU ARE GOING

In Part 2, we explore where you are going. You might use the four states of "matter" as a metaphor for remaining agile as you pursue what "matters" most in your life. Living a life that matters requires the stability of a solid plan that becomes flexible as you go with the flow of daily life. Along the way, you will feel the need to accelerate specific areas where movement is needed. This acceleration will come through the language you use. The final state of getting where you want to go is sparking the collective movement of others through the power of autosuggestion.

THE FOUR STATES OF MATTER—
FOUR STATES THAT MATTER

solids *liquids* *gases* *plasmas*

Principle	State	Feeling	Desired Result
Your Plan	Solids	Being concrete	Stability
Visualization	Liquids	Going with the flow	Flexibility
Language Creates Reality	Gases	Accelerating	Movement
Autosuggestion	Plasmas	Sparking	Collective movement

Again, natural laws provide a simple pattern for getting where you want to go.

HOW YOU WILL GET THERE

Start anywhere, go everywhere—North, South, East and West. Grow in every direction. Be intentional about where you are in relation to your True North. Be prepared for crisis when things go South. Look both ways—observe the wisdom from the East and the abundance of the West as you seek inspiration for your life. As you move toward where you are going, you will not follow a straight line. In Part 3, you will begin moving towards your new horizon.

NORTH

WEST   **EAST**

SOUTH

Principle	Direction	Feeling	Desired Result
Be Intentional	North	Alignment with your true north	A deep sense of purpose
Be Abundant	West	There is enough for everyone	Independence and prosperity
Go Exponential	East	Being conscious	Spiritual growth
Prepare for Crisis	South	Being alert	Character growth

In the first part of this book, you will learn **where you are now** and apply four principles for growing your value-add: 1) *Trust*—Build trust with yourself and others; 2) *Freedom*—Choose your attitude; 3) *Gratitude*—Become thankful, and 4) Self-Confidence—Be at peace with yourself. Knowing where you are now in relation to these four foundational growth principles will prepare you for accelerated growth, both personally and professionally.

In the second part of this book, **where you are going** will become clear. You will learn and apply four principles of vision and big thinking: 5) *Your Plan*—Achieve meaningful goals; 6) *Visualization*—Shape your future; 7) *Language Creates Reality*—Inspire people, and 8) *Autosuggestion*—Tap into fresh power. By applying these four principles, you will explore and see new and exciting horizons.

In Part 3, you will learn **how to get where you hope to go** and apply four principles for doing what it takes to reach your next horizon: 9) *Be Intentional*—Reaching your horizon; 10) *Be Abundant*—Inviting others to your horizon; 11) *Go Exponential*—Seeking synergy, and 12) *Prepare for Crisis*—Walking beyond the runway.

The life-long journey of creating yourself and growing your unique contribution culminates in your life's legacy. Knowing where you are now, where you are going and how you will get there is a simple and repeatable pattern for continuously creating value.

SEE, DO AND GROW

Several times a year we both arrive on Tuesday morning at the Park Weggis Hotel in Weggis, Switzerland. We are there to coach scientists and executives of one of the world's largest and most valuable companies—leaders who have made it to the top of their field. They all have completed a 360° profile on their leadership behavior. In their profile, their managers, peers, direct reports and other stakeholders all give them feedback on their leadership behavior and adherence to the company's values and principles. We assist them in identifying strengths and understanding the personal legacy that they have established within the company.

Having conducted hundreds of coaching sessions with leaders worldwide, we notice that leaders tend to skip directly to the last few pages of their profile, read what has been written about how they can better develop themselves, and then begin "doing." The dominant mindset is to do more.

Most participants tend to thank the people who are providing the feedback and promise to work on the areas of development that were highlighted. They might say: "Thank you for taking the time to complete my profile. I agree that I need to work on my communication," or "I have some ideas for improving this area of my leadership." Most participants then start privately guessing about what they can do to improve their communication. Many even begin making changes to their behavior, only to discover their stakeholders do not SEE what they DO in relationship to their feedback in the profile. Therefore, the participant's brand, and more importantly their opportunities to contribute, do not GROW.

A more powerful approach is to focus on personal and professional strengths and the results you are achieving rather than the flaws. This approach sounds like this: "Thank you for taking the time to complete my profile. I understand that you value and appreciate my technical expertise and other areas of strength. Thank you for recognizing how important getting the science right has been to the results we have achieved with this project. I specifically liked your written comment, making the connections between this project and its relevance to our five-year strategy. With regard to communication, I learned that you would like me to be more present in discussions with my peers. May I ask, what does *excellent communication* with my peers look like to you? Where would you recommend I start? Which discussions most need my presence?"

Be aware of how people SEE your brand and then DO the things that GROW your brand: SEE, DO, GROW. Our experience as implementation architects designing change processes suggests that about 90% of managers spend most of their time and energy DOING. In fact, they're so busy DOING, they don't take time to SEE new horizons and opportunities.

About 5% of the managers have *dreams*, meaning they SEE new opportunities but do not DO anything concrete to realize them.

Only about 5% of managers both SEE and DO. These are the real performers. They have learned the profound principle of seeing before doing to accelerate growth.

We find strength-based leadership more satisfying to leaders than simply focusing on development areas. Many executives are surprised when we do not focus on their weaknesses and the corresponding "to-do" lists they have created. The room changes as their mindset shifts from dealing with a small weakness to exploring the possibility of making a bigger difference. The conversation often goes from one of concern and a sense of heaviness to one of fun and lightness filled with new possibilities. Leaders' body language becomes visibly more animated as they see why their life matters as *human beings*. Many of them are tired of all the *human doing* they are trying to sustain. The idea of seeing new horizons and engaging in fun, meaningful work that makes a unique difference is exciting.

Seeing then doing will *grow* your brand, and boost the joy that you find in your life. Change really is possible—not only on the surface but also at depth: you can truly shape your character in a positive and permanent manner. Regardless of how your life has been in the past—regardless of success, defeat, pain, joy, grief, trauma and dreams—you can change. The past is past! You have the choice to design the future effectively now! Change means seeing new horizons and then doing fun, meaningful things in small steps. *Life is not about finding yourself—it's about creating yourself.*

Change, fulfillment, success, power—all this is possible. While reading this book, you have a wonderful chance to create your life with renewed vigor.

CHARACTERISTICS OF LIVE WITH INTENT

We acknowledge that thousands of books have already been written on these topics. The bottleneck of society today is not a lack of information; to the contrary, we are overwhelmed by the diversity of data and information on most subjects. This phenomenon is not new. Back in 1612 Spanish playwright, Lope de Vega wrote: *"So many books—so much confusion! To send us a printed ocean, that for the most part is covered with froth."*[1]

What would de Vega say today?

This book is organized in a way that enables you to learn the various skills in an easy and enjoyable manner. You will get plenty of instructions and background information in order to *put the principles into practice;* because, in the end, that is what really matters.

In each chapter, you will be guided and prompted to apply proven success principles in a systematic and clear manner, step by step, and at your own pace. Our method is holistic. You will receive all necessary instructions on how to transfer the methods into practice.

HOW TO BENEFIT MOST FROM THIS BOOK

Here are six specific ways to benefit most from reading this book:

1. Prepare a calm place where you can read with concentration. The chapters are designed to make reading easier. Today, due to digitalization, the simplest of all learning activities—reading—has been pushed into the background. The ubiquitous "multitasking"—doing several things at once—has destroyed thoughtful reflection and distorted thinking in general. You will develop outstanding talents and qualities

---

1   Lope de Vega, *Alle Bürger sind Soldaten*, see Michael Olmert: *The Smithsonian Book of Books*, Smithsonian Books, Washington, 1992, p. 301

when you develop the ability to "concentrate on one." Organize a calm place where you can read with concentration, repeat the passages, and absorb this accumulated knowledge. *What you do, do with your whole heart and soul. There is no glory in half-heartedness.* This adage is still true today.

2. Read each paragraph attentively and ponder it afterward. You will want to read through these principles differently than you would read a newspaper or magazine. To integrate the principles into your life, you need to digest the information and reflect on it. Be actively involved in reading the passages. Take a pen and underline the paragraphs, sentences, and words that are meaningful to you. Make notes and answer the questions in writing so that through your study and active involvement, the book becomes a personal development tool. Imagine what opportunities you might have grasped had you completed *Live with Intent* earlier in your life. Imagine the challenges you might have solved with more force and clarity!

3. Take your time. Take your time while *creating your future* on your personal journey to greater success. What matters most is not how fast you read through these materials, but how thoroughly and methodically you work through them. Take each chapter in turn and move on to the next chapter only when you feel that you have completed all of the tasks and internalized all of the information of the previous chapter. You will then achieve momentum and progress faster. The chapters flow in a logical, sequential manner; when you follow the prescribed procedures, you will achieve remarkable results and develop highly effective habits.

4. Be diligent. Work for at least seven days applying the exercises of each chapter before you read on. Concentrate on only one chapter at a time. The techniques, tips, and affirmations should be practiced every day. When these exercises are diligently practiced, they will improve various aspects of your life and bring you closer to your goals.

5. Be you (authenticity). Our clients are extraordinarily diverse in their professions—entrepreneurs, students, engineers, medical representatives, freelancers, top managers, craftsmen, board members, housewives, pensioners, employees and self-employed people from all walks of life—but they all have one thing in common: They are well-grounded with a strong desire to move forward in life.

6. Seek real success. Because this growth process is based on verified psychological principles, it enables you to acquire the techniques and properties quickly, without interrupting your daily routine. As you apply these principles into daily practice, they become second nature to you. And, you will soon experience remarkable and effective results. You will discover the key to being very successful lies *within you*; you have the potential to be even more successful than you ever dreamed possible. To us, being *successful* means that you stand out from the anonymous crowd as you create a deeply meaningful life of contribution.

Part 1

Where You Are Now

YOUR PROGRESS MUST START HERE.

> ## "START AT THE VERY BEGINNING, A VERY GOOD PLACE TO START."
>
> ~Lyric from the *"Sound of Music."*

In this first section, we explore the question "Where are you now?" and introduce four foundational principles: Trust, Freedom, Gratitude, and Self-Confidence.

CHAPTER 1

Trust: Build trust with yourself and others

CHAPTER 2

Freedom: Choose your attitude

CHAPTER 3

Gratitude: Become thankful

CHAPTER 4

Self-Confidence: Be at peace with yourself

CHAPTER 1
TRUST

BUILD TRUST WITH YOURSELF AND OTHERS

SUCCESS AND **HAPPINESS ARE NOT SUBJECT TO** COINCIDENCE—THEY ARE **AFTER-EFFECTS.**

Life is demanding by design. No one makes it through life without being tested.

Within every human being is a story that includes struggle. **THE STRUGGLE IS THE STORY.**

The only way to fully experience and appreciate the **HIGHS IN LIFE** is to be familiar with the lows.

Like long winters create a craving for spring, **trusting your life** matters creates a craving for making a unique contribution.

Trust, symbolized by winter, is the first principle of *Live with Intent.* Winter time is when we turn inside and build **OUR RE-**

SERVES. When building trust, the best place to start is with **YOU**. This is where you have the most **INFLUENCE**. If you don't trust yourself, you are less likely to trust others. Meanwhile, trusting others is no guarantee they will trust you. When others do trust you, **be grateful**, follow their lead and trust yourself even more.

SELF-TRUST means that deep down you know **your life matters**. You feel the value you create **makes a difference**. Trusting yourself and your ability to create unique value, regardless of how cold or long the winter, is your deepest source of **STRENGTH** and continually growing your Value-Add is your greatest asset.

Thomas*:* From reading Stephen R. Covey's bestselling book, *The 7 Habits of Highly Effective People*, I had a good grasp of the concept of trust. His pragmatic definitions of trust and trustworthiness made sense to me. Little did I know at the time that life would continue to teach me deep lessons about trust.

When our first child, our son Kai, was one month old we were somewhat astonished that his diapers were not filled with urine. We had no clue what he was going through. For four weeks, Kai's kidneys were being flooded with urine since he had a "reflux" condition where the tube connecting the kidneys to the bladder was working both ways.

We became alarmed when we found blood in his diaper. Doctors examined him, and told us the bad news: to discover the extent of the damage to the kidneys caused by the "reflux," they would need to perform a multiple-hour surgery. The back of Kai's left kidney was so hard that he had to drill through it—and it was functioning under 10%.

We then visited with several experts and hospitals and learned that we had two options:

Option 1: Dr. Metzger (in German, *Metzger* means *butcher*) was convinced that one of the kidneys, if not both, needed to be removed immediately! Dr. Metzger was very experienced in this kind of surgery—he had real competence. He told us that once he made an incision, he would then see what else needed fixing. Even though Dr. Metzger was high on competence, we felt terrible.

Option 2: Dr. Kamran was one of the nicest persons I have ever met in my life. He was so kind, so considerate—a gentle and spiritual man. He said that he would "treat Kai as if he were his own son." As a family, we could feel his sincerity, and we believed him. This man had character. We felt great around him… until we asked, "How often do you perform this surgery?" He replied, "Only once or twice a year."

So the decision was between competence and character. Which option would you choose? To which doctor would you entrust the life of your son at four weeks of age?

Please ponder this question, since this is the key to understanding trust.

The confluence of competence and character creates trustworthiness. Through interaction, trustworthiness can turn into trust. Trustworthiness and trust are like fragile plants; they need care and nurturing to thrive. Plants that never seem to get enough water, never seem to have the right spot of sun or climate. Plants that cannot seem to get "settled in" are comparable to people lacking the conditions of trust.

What did we do with Kai? We ensured a strong cooperation of both experts. We did not accept competence or character only. That was a good start in helping Kai with his health challenges. In the 20 surgeries that followed, Dr. Kamran's gifted hand and caring heart especially ensured Kai's survival. To him, we are forever indebted.

It was, however, always a matter of walking a fine line, striving for the balance of character and competence in all treatments that Kai received. To the doctors, our many questions and requests must have seemed excessive—like we were being *difficult* or thought that we were *"extra special"*— but we knew that building trust was not dependent on one factor alone. The experience was one of the most fundamental learnings in my life so far.

Over many years Justin and I worked with the late Stephen R. Covey and his son Stephen M.R. Covey. The concepts of personal trustworthiness in Stephen M.R.'s book *The Speed of Trust* have become part of our DNA. Hence, we have made Trust the first principle of *Live with Intent*. As you build self-trust, character and competence are two of the main elements. In teaching and implementing this principle, we have come to the realization trust is the foundation principle enabling our quest of living a life that matters.

Justin: In the winter of 2005, business failure haunted me. I could not focus on work beyond mid-morning. By 10 a.m., I needed to get away from the depression filling my office and get outside. I spent hours wandering aimlessly through the forests near our house in Belgium. For several weeks, I can still remember the traffic noise of the E411 freeway giving way to the quiet stillness of the Solgnes Forest as I faded into the woods. The smell of dampness as mist surrounded my face from breathing the cold air. I was lost and discouraged. Tears of discouragement flowed easily. We had invested our life savings into our dream business that failed. Financially and emotionally broken, I had to come to grips with my dream not working out. My family had trusted that I would succeed, and I had let them down.

Trying to stay calm and one step ahead of the debilitating fear of surviving financially, I doubted myself, my abilities, and my purpose in life. I lost sight of my talents and could no longer see why my life mattered.

I am grateful for my wife's encouragement and for Thomas who gave me perspective. "Pull yourself together," he told me. "Doctors who spend half their life training to be world-class doctors have a duty to share their competency with the world. You have spent your whole life training to inspire people to live lives that matter. This is your competency and duty. Stay focused, don't give up. If you run out of money, you can come and live at my house. If you stop chasing your dream of doing fun and meaningful work, you won't be able to live with yourself."

It took me three years to let go of the anger that was dulling my sense of purpose. I had to rebuild the trust I had in myself and other people. I had to revisit my own character and competence: Who did I want to be as a person? What were my values? What were my talents? What was my life all about? I had to take it one day at a time, recognizing and celebrating my small successes.

This experience was a refiner's fire, purifying my character and sense of purpose. I came away from it seeing a clear pattern for helping myself and others live lives that matter. I realized that I am uniquely competent in helping people live more meaningful lives. With this realization, I began trusting myself with my own talents and genius. As a result of my own resolve and sense of self-trust, I was able to generate trust with many people in well-known organizations. Today, most of my professional life is doing fun, meaningful work that makes a difference.

Life Lesson: Trusting yourself and others are the foundations of a purpose-driven life.

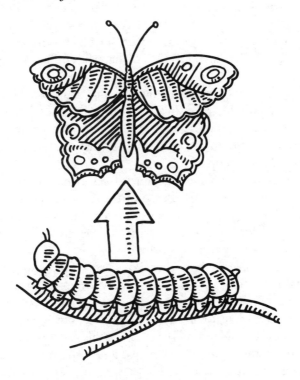

Thomas: As I finished a personal consultation with the board member of a listed company, I looked out his office window to the factory gate below. Many of the staff had finished their work for the day and were passing through the impressive railings on their way home. These employees were just an average group of individuals, yet some of them had chosen to walk a more defined path. Their lives would be more successful than those of their colleagues.

We often see people who, as if lifted by an unseen hand, stand out and create a far more impressive future than the contemporaries with whom they rub shoulders. How is that done?

Have you asked yourself: Why do some people have so much more success than others?

Conventional answers—successful people have more luck than others, are more talented, or receive decisively more advantages from family connections or birth—did not satisfy me. I was always convinced that we had the ability to shape our own lives.

On closer inspection, the lives of successful people actually teach us something completely different. The determining factors of success, failure or mediocrity are neither genetically nor environmentally governed; nor are they by-products of the number of offered opportunities.

Successful people owe their success neither to owning exceptional abilities nor to chance but to a planned order of life. Even the most ordinary people can achieve remarkable success and fortune—if they trust and develop the aptitudes and abilities they naturally possess!

Many people believe they are successful or at least on the path to success. In reality, they are comfortable and only spectators to success. Some people may understand intellectually what it takes to be successful, but in many cases, they are on the sidelines. They can't fathom taking the actual steps to get there; instead, they just languish on the sidelines, dwelling on ideas and wishes that never get implemented. In the words of Rabindranath Tagore: "I have spent my days stringing and unstringing my instrument, while the song I came to sing remains unsung." Without trust in a deeper sense of purpose, their actions become inconsistent and ineffective, so they are relegated to an observer status, never singing the song they came to sing.

By applying these timeless principles not just once but as an ongoing process, you will have access to all the necessary skills and self-trust to become a remarkable athlete in the game of life.

The laws of success are universal—much like the laws of nature. They apply to everyone. The consequence of applying these laws differentiates achievement from failure. The path to success starts with self-trust. This trust leads to knowing and feeling that you matter, which will lead to trust that every life matters, that every life has value to add.

If we are passionate about being successful, we will come to the realization that adding value to the lives of others is life's greatest source of lasting joy. Start defining yourself by the value you create for and with other people.

Do fun, meaningful work. While we all need to stand alone and be comfortable with who we are, where we are going, and what we are achieving along the way, living a life that matters requires us to trust others and to be trusted by others. Not once over the past 20 years of helping others live lives that matter have we ever found someone who could get what they wanted, what they really wanted, without trusting others. Think about it, can you get what you want independent of other people? Can you have fun, meaningful work independent of other people?

We are like aspen trees. Entire groves of aspen trees are actually one single living organism sharing the same root system. Like aspen trees, people are interconnected. We have a common root system. Every tree has a unique story. We all have unique stories. Inside we find the tree's story. Inside ourselves, we find our own stories. Trees have scars; people have scars. Each year a tree's growth is marked by an additional ring; when you cut a tree in half, you can see that some years are better than others.

Year by year, we grow, we continually create our future. Achieving what we want most in life requires connections with others. At some point, we begin seeing ourselves within a forest where everything is interconnected. Like aspen groves, our lives are connected to those around us. We share a common root system. Our success is connected to other's success.

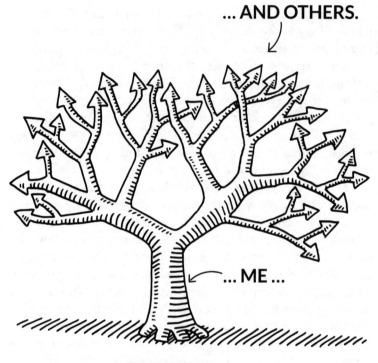

... AND OTHERS.

... ME ...

TRUSTING ...

Trust is the deepest form of a root system connecting people. Without it, we cannot survive. With it, our opportunities for doing fun, meaningful work are limitless.

From a business perspective, *doing work without meaning* is what Brent Peterson and Gaylan Nielson call "Fake work." Fake work happens when we lose sight of our horizon and spend our time wandering and working without purpose.

Fake work destroys self-trust. It is not fun and can be stopped immediately. Fake work is pretending—pretending we enjoy our work, pretending we enjoy the people we work with, and pretending we are adding value to the world. Pretending drains the life out of us, diminishing our sense of purpose and killing our productivity. Fake work leads us away from our horizons and leads to burnout. Fake work leaves us tired and unfulfilled. Fun, meaningful work leading to our horizons can leave us tired but fulfilled. Fun, meaningful work creates self-trust, a sense of contribution that attracts others to your horizon. In organizations, eliminating fake work is one of the best things we can do to build a culture of high trust.

When we consult on trust, we pose this question: "I need you to help me with a serious problem. You may not see your family or sleep much for several weeks."

Interestingly, we always get the same response. "What is the problem? What is in it for me? Who benefits from solving the problem?" Eventually, someone will ask: "Who is asking for help?"

We respond with pictures of people that the local audience will recognize. For example, what if the person asking were Bono from the band U2? What if the person were Donald Trump? How about Pope Francis, Steve Jobs, Barack Obama, Angela Merkel or Nelson Mandela?

As soon as people see the picture or hear the name of who is asking, the answer is instantaneous. What creates such an immediate answer? Trust. Almost like a sixth sense, we make immediate judgments about who we trust. The bigger question is who trusts you? How long does it take people to decide if they will follow you?

Trust is contagious. When building trust, you can start anywhere and go everywhere. As depicted in the *Trust Development Cycle* graph, you have many ways to enter the trust development cycle. If others trust you, it is easier to trust yourself. If you trust yourself, it is easier to trust others. The more you trust others, the more others will trust you.

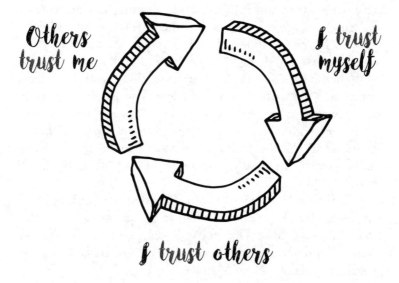

Others trust me

I trust myself

I trust others

The best place to start is to trust yourself. This trust is where you have the most influence. If you don't trust yourself, you are less likely to trust others. Meanwhile, trusting others does not guarantee they will trust you. When others trust you, be grateful, follow their lead and trust yourself even more.

TRANSFER INTO PRACTICE (TIP)

Each chapter ends with a *Transfer Into Practice* (TIP) section, comprised of **SEE, DO** and **GROW** applications, along with **Affirmations** and **Checklists**.

SEE—See the type of person you wish to become. Record your impressions. Describe the pictures that come into your mind's eye as you concentrate on this exercise.

DO—Before you fall asleep tonight, imagine the type of person you want to become. The person you can evolve to if you follow this method with discipline. Keep this image with you until you are asleep; this will then be imprinted into your subconscious. Repeat this valuable exercise in visualization for eight consecutive nights to enable your brain to create a "folder" that documents your development and re-instates your desire for change.

> *"Dare to dream of what you are not.*
> *Dare to dream of what you have not.*
> *Dare to dream as you really are,*
> *Awake and keep the dreamlike impression of your true self."*
> ~ *Margot Bickel*

GROW—Growth is the result of seeing and doing. To boost your growth, start using a **Learning Journal** to record your growth. Write your thoughts, goals, feelings, successes, and failures—anything that impacts you on your journey. This journal will be your personal guidebook to climbing those summits of successes that are important to you. In later years, your impressions will be an important memory jogger for you.

You might implement a color system for your learning, such as *thoughts* in black; *feelings* in blue; *findings* and *insights* in red; *achievements* in green, etc.

Affirmations

At the end of every chapter, you will receive examples of formulas/affirmations that actively shape and reinforce what you SEE, which heavily influences what you DO. You can integrate these affirmations into your daily life by reading them often during the day. You can write little sticky notes and put them all over the house—for example—on the bathroom mirror, in the kitchen on the refrigerator, on your calendar, or by the phone. The more you see, the more you do.

These six affirmations will accelerate your growth:
- You make good decisions. Your pathway to success is visible to yourself.
- You look forward to your journey, which is just beginning now.
- You find safety within yourself and within your chosen path of *shaping your future.*
- The success in your life is increasing.
- You are going the right way. Everything will be fine, as you trust in your new skills.
- This is your time. Your time has come. Step by step your pathway to success reveals itself.

Affirmations are covered in more detail in Chapter 8. There we discuss the powerful technique of *autosuggestion*, the effective programming of our subconscious mind. Until then, please take these affirmations as an impetus for positive thoughts.

CHAPTER 2

FREEDOM

CHOOSE YOUR ATTITUDE

WHATEVER YOU CAN DO, OR DREAM YOU CAN DO, BEGIN IT. BOLDNESS HAS GENIUS, POWER, AND MAGIC IN IT. BEGIN IT NOW.

JOHANN WOLFGANG
VON GOETHE

Freedom, symbolized by spring, is the second principle of *Live with Intent*. Spring time is when we **BLOSSOM** and **PROACTIVELY RENEW our unique contributions**. This is when we stretch ourselves and grow our abilities and when we manifest the character we are building. Being proactive means taking full **RESPONSIBILITY** for our lives and the **contributions we make to the world**. Independent of external influences, proactive people live life on their own terms.

The **HAPPINESS you feel** and the freedom you enjoy flow from the choices **YOU make**. Like springtime, proactivity offers **NEW LIFE—THE LIFE YOU CREATE.** Winter always yields to spring. Each year brings **new opportunities to explore, discover and grow.** The opportunity to create new life every year **keeps us fresh, renewed and ALIVE**.

Today, **VALUES and personal morals** are often viewed as irrelevant or unattractive, not praiseworthy or desirable. This attitude manifests itself in our families, companies, clubs, societies and the media. **RESPONSIBILITY** is dismissed or elegantly disguised, and actions are too often subject to the vulnerability of the moment. Thus, our **cultural reflexes** are predominantly reactive. They are even reactive in a contagious way since it is easier to react to the current predominant **FEELINGS** around us than to to be proactive. Often, when we are reactive, peer pressure and the desire to belong to the group unite with a "common enemy" distinction towards whom we are reactive to; which gives **THE INDIVIDUAL the impression of being better** than the rest but still belonging to the crowd. An **ENVIRONMENT** that makes being proactive is not the obvious choice.

Thomas: Justin and I started a consulting company with two other partners in 2001. The goal of the company was to align people and organizations with purpose. Teaching people the value of trust and how to create it in the workplace was at the heart of our approach. So it was a real shock for our team when we, the owners, found ourselves divided from one day to the next due to various petty conflicts; we no longer trusted each other. After years of effort to build up the company, we had new employees trained and new customers steadily streaming in when dissention from within threatened to capsize our business.

We were reminded of the adage, "Ships don't sink because of the water around them. They sink because of the water that gets in them." Our business was taking on water fast. The four principal players involved in the first phase of growing the Reichart Leadership Group were in conflict. We had become preoccupied with ourselves, rather than the needs of our customers. The company, our employees' jobs, our ability to repay investors became vulnerable and in danger of disappearing. The team and the company stood on the precipice of collapse. Had it not been for one person, Justin, the company would have plummeted into financial ruin.

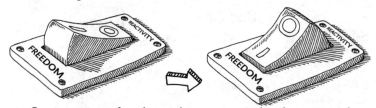

Justin managed to keep the team together long enough to keep our commitments to customers and repay our external investors. How did he do it? Over the years Justin had cultivated a ***proactive mindset***.

He had developed self-beliefs like:
I have the freedom to choose my attitude.
I concentrate on my circle of influence.
I act consistently with my values, even under adverse circumstances.

I am accountable for my own area of responsibility.
I do not participate in speculation or recrimination.
I am, and always will be, responsible for my actions.

Justin had a calming influence; he didn't get carried away with the petty troubles of the moment; he didn't give in to concerns; he was a tower of strength that stayed focused on customers and prevented the team from tumbling over.

Instead of avoiding responsibility and participating in the blame game, Justin used his influence to broker agreements with me and the other two partners. It was not easy managing egos, broken dreams and future needs. The agreement included me peacefully leaving the company—the company with my name on it! While it did not feel great at the time, I credited Justin for the company surviving long enough to deliver on its commitments. In our moment of crisis, Justin's proactive attitude made all the difference.

* * *

This scenario may seem simplified and exaggerated, but it isn't! By moving from *Reactive* to *Proactive* mode, we can stop the flow of negative energy—even reverse it—and start a contagious positive and creative energy.

To be *reactive* means:
- Giving in to our moods, feelings, appetites, and passions
- Aligning our behavior with external forces and conditions
- Blaming our actions on our circumstances
- Apportioning blame or shame to others
- Concentrating on the weaknesses of others
- Abdicating responsibility for our choices

When we practice reactive behavior, we entangle ourselves emotionally. We lose our ability to act and succumb to our own interests and feelings. We are no longer true to ourselves.

We are reacting to external forces. There is no space between the *stimulus* that comes from outside influences and our own responses. In this situation, there is no freedom to act according to our values. Our behavior is instinctive. Like animals, we respond to a stimulus with reactive instincts. Similarly, some people are bound to their emotions and impulses and thus forfeit the freedom to choose how they respond to a stimulus. They are not willing or able to choose their actions.

The fruits of such behavior are common: addiction; broken relationships; grief; excessive anger; aggression; injury; fear; loneliness; loss of confidence; and extreme mood swings.

> *"It's not what happens to us, but our response to what happens to us that hurts us."*
> ~ Stephen R. Covey, author, The 7 Habits of Highly Effective People

From Victim to Creator

The good news is this: ***You have a choice!*** To be reactive is a choice and a decision. You can stop responding that way and change your lifestyle. If you choose a path of self-responsibility and living by your own values, you're making a choice to embrace true freedom. Find your way out of powerlessness and on to the road to personal power through the ability to shape the course of your life yourself.

The opposite of reactive action is proactive action. Being proactive does not mean an excess of activity, energy, and power, but rather a conscious decision to be the captain of your own soul and act upon your values and principles.

In business, the company **The Body Shop** lives this principle extraordinarily. The company sells more than 1,200 hair and body care products in 2,500 shops in 62 countries.[1]

---

1   See www.thebodyshop.de, Unser Unternehmen, http://www.thebodyshop.com/about-us/aboutus_company.aspx, accessed on 08/27/2015

The retailer chain had a turnover of about 1.4 billion euros in 2014.[2]

The Body Shop follows its **five core values** consistently: Community Trade; human rights; animal welfare; self-respect and environmental protection[3]. These values are put into practice through the Body Shop's incorporated "Help by Trade" program, which is operated by more than 30 suppliers from 20 countries worldwide. For example, the Marula oil project in Namibia was designed to help make women more self-sufficient. In that program, the women of the Eudafano Women's Cooperative sow the seeds of the fruit by hand and let the oil of the seeds squeeze coldly at the factory. Three kilos of oil are enough to buy a school uniform and textbooks for one year.[4] Participants always receive a fair wage, and often a "social premium" of 10 percent as a bonus to fund projects of the municipality, usually in the fields of education, health or water supplies.[5]

Due to the program, the women have become more self-confident, courageous and independent. The goal is not to push sales or to shine on an economic level, but to improve the "social and ecological conversion."[6] **Anita Roddick**, the now deceased foundress, once said: "I would prefer to be judged by how I treat the weaker and threatened communities with whom I do business, rather than at the height of my profit margin.

---

2   See www.statista.com, Umsatz von The Body Shop im Einzelhandel weltweit in den Jahren 2010 bis 2014 (in Millionen Euro), http://de.statista.com/statistik/daten/studie/255799/umfrage/umsatz-von-the-body-shop/, accessed on 08/27/2015

3   See www.thebodyshop.com, Our Company, http://www.thebodyshop.com/about-us/aboutus_company.aspx, accessed on 08/27/2015

4   See www.thebodyshop.de, values, http://www.thebodyshop.de/werte/inhaltsstoff-marulaoel.aspx, accessed on 08/27/2015, cf. Roddick, A., Die Body Shop Story. Die Vision einer aussergewöhnlichen Unternehmerin, Munich 2001, p. 230ff.

5   See Roddick, A., Die Body Shop Story. Die Vision einer aussergewöhnlichen Unternehmerin, Munich 2001, p. 239

6   See Roddick, A., Die Body Shop Story. Die Vision einer aussergewöhnlichen Unternehmerin, Munich 2001, p. 240

If all of us who are in business would accept this principle, really great things could happen. At least in this regard—if not elsewhere—applies the saying 'small is beautiful.'"[7]

Anita Roddick and The Body Shop are bringing modest prosperity to remote and impoverished areas of the world in this sustainable fashion. They work in their sphere of activity and combine business interests, cosmetic products and development assistance in an exciting approach. We think The Body Shop is a clear example of what being proactive means: to focus on what we feel is important, to stay focused on our values and legacy, rather than to immerse "head-down" in short term needs and press quick-fix solutions, which tend to be reactive in nature.

How Does Proactivity Play Out?

If we are proactive, then our actions will not be influenced by the guilt trips, manipulations or influences of others. Regardless of the decisions and actions of other people, we make decisions in accordance and in conjunction with our values, projects and visions. We are in alignment with our concerns and ourselves; we understand our needs and desires. We are on a direct path to achieve our desires and goals; we cannot be distracted or unnecessarily stopped from achieving that which we have set our mind and heart upon.

To a certain degree, you can't be manipulated.

The *cause-and-effect principle* teaches us: reactive behavior is responding to an outside influence; proactive behavior produces a different result. We are the decision makers—we are the stimulus that causes the action, not something in the outside world.

Just as a muscle must be trained, so must our "proactive muscle" be trained in order to continuously produce a proactive attitude. A strong *proactive muscle* will produce these results:

---

7   See Roddick, A., Die Body Shop Story. Die Vision einer aussergewöhnlichen Unternehmerin, Munich 2001, p. 240

- You achieve **your** goals.
- You assume full responsibility for your decisions and behavior.
- You act in accordance with what is most important to you.
- You act according to your personal vision and mission.
- You are at one with yourself and feel your own freedom, purpose and power.
- Your energy is focused on your direct area of influence within you and around you.

The more proactive you are, the more effective you are. Your actions are more orientated toward your horizon and thus achieve new levels of success. As you develop the characteristic of proactivity, you more clearly see and benefit from the time between the stimulus and response.

Viktor Frankl demonstrated an impressive example of proactive behavior. During World War II he was a prisoner in a concentration camp; after he was released, he wrote several books about what he had observed and used his experiences in his psychotherapy work. He calls attitude the last of the human freedoms: "We who lived in the concentration camps can remember the men who walked through the huts comforting others, giving away their last piece of bread. They may have been few in number, but they offer sufficient proof that everything can be taken from a man but one thing: the last of the human freedoms—to choose one's attitude in any given set of circumstances, to choose one's own way."[8]

During our lives, we have each met several genuinely remarkable and highly successful individuals who have assumed personal responsibility over and above the norm, and in each case, the person's proactive attitude became the cornerstone of his or her success.

Reactive people often reap unwanted results through impulsive behavior. These results are generally contrary to the desired objective!

Consider your own life's experiences. Do you like to spend your free time with reactive people? Is it enjoyable to work with reactive colleagues or a reactive boss? No!

Proactive people surprise you with their ability to generate value for people, families, and projects. They are reliable and productive. Make the choice to be proactive.

---

8   Frankl, Viktor E., *Man's Search for Meaning*, Beacon Press, Boston, 1959, p. 65–66

TIP

The following exercises will help you assess your habits in terms of being proactive or reactive when it comes to what language you choose and how you take care of your body.

Your Language

SEE—Distinguish between your proactive and reactive language. This requires special attention; it is crucial, because "language creates reality." Here you will see examples of both forms.

Proactive language	Reactive language
"I want to go."	"I have to go."
"I will do."	"I have to do."
"It may be wise to explore ..."	"If only I could."
"What options do we have?"	"I cannot do anything."
"I will ..."	"I should; I must ..."
"I am concerned about ..."	"This is an outrage!"

DO

A. Practice proactive language

Continue with the list of examples above and focus on replacing reactive language with proactive language. Watch what happens when you only use a proactive vocabulary.

B. Personal observation (reflection)

Identify situations in which you tend to be reactive. Briefly, describe the situations. What events trigger your reactions? What goes through your mind when these triggers occur? What do you say to yourself in response to these triggers?

Find out the *trigger* that led to the situation mentioned above and the reactive response. What circumstances, moods, and feelings triggered your reaction?

1. What was the result of your reactive behavior? Did it correspond with your expectations and goals? What were the causes of it? What was the cost for you in terms of relationships, the trust factor?
2. How do you feel now when you think back on it?
3. How would the results have been different if you had acted proactively instead of reactively?
4. Now invent a different ending—one that is in harmony with your values and horizon.
5. In your example, was there space for a thought-out, deliberate response? What would have helped you to act proactively instead of reactively? What answer would correspond more with your values?
6. Now, look at the last situation in your life in which you behaved in a way that you were not proud of. Examine this situation carefully and then think—perhaps even write down—what you could have done in order to achieve more personal freedom by being proactive.

YOUR BODY

"Health is the first duty in life." ~ Oscar Wilde

SEE—An important indicator of how well we are managing the characteristic of responsibility begins at the physical level; indeed your own body will reveal your attitude to you. How mature are you with your own physical freedom regarding your body? How well do you treat yourself?

What do you eat? How good is the quality of the food you buy, prepare, and eat?

Ask yourself: "Do I give my body the same attention and professional care as I give my car?"

In order to improve your strength, maintain effectiveness and thereby train your proactive muscle, you need to choose good food and nourishment consciously. Doing so means you will develop more mental strength and vigor and you will be able to look forward to many hours, days, weeks and years with a healthy body.

How responsible are you regarding this precious gift of life that you have received? How well do you treat your healthy, functioning body?

"He, who wants to stay strong, healthy and young for as long as possible, be moderate, exercise the body, breathe pure air and heal sorrows by fasting rather than by medication!"
~ Hippocrates, 460 BC–370 BC

Nutrition, Exercise, and Rhythm

You need to act responsibly without compromising in three areas of your life:

1) *Nutrition*	
2) *Exercise*	
3) *Rhythm*	

An optimum implementation of these three areas will result in a stable and healthy lifestyle. It will ensure that you not only have a basically healthy life but a clear head and a positive mental attitude—all of which will strengthen your resolve.

How are you doing? Can you afford to continue with the status quo?

Nutrition. This transfer exercise will give you some tips that you can also apply to how you approach nutrition. You'll eventually have new experiences with the subject of nutrition, so stick to the new positive habits!

Exercise. You will pay a high price if exercise is not already part of your lifestyle. Physical exercise is the key to energy, strength, and relaxation. Activity improves psychological and mental agility.

Rhythm. Treat yourself to a *rhythmic life.* In other words, treat yourself to a life of stable patterns and reliable conscious investments towards yourself. As Rudolf Steiner says, *"Rhythm gives birth to life."* In nature, all life processes are rhythmic. Our sleeping and waking patterns are the largest body rhythm that we have, but inhaling and exhaling are also a natural rhythm, as well as the body's release of the smallest amounts of enzymes or hormones. Everything is subject to repetition. Your working day should also be subject to rhythms or patterns—phases of tension or stress should be followed by phases of relaxation.

You should plan these rhythms of work and relaxation into your weekly routine.

Go to sleep at the same time every day, and eat your meals at fixed times every day, if possible. Give your body this treat. A structured, patterned life gives you an immense power. Again and again, we have to deal with stress and change, and life will have its crises! In order to be ready for future crises, you need to prepare now. Most healthy and successful people we know have a very simple rhythm: they go to bed early and get up early in the morning!

Early to bed, early to rise, makes a man healthy, wealthy and wise. When Pope John Paul II was asked how at his advanced age, he could manage the immense workload that was demanded of his office, he replied dryly, "I sleep at night"!

The World Health Organization defines health as follows: *"Health is a state of complete physical, mental and social well-being, not merely the absence of disease or infirmity."*[9]

Start today by making healthy choices. Choose to invest in your body (you only have this one) and in so doing you will increase the chances of enjoying a long and healthy life.

> *"In the first half of life we sacrifice our health to earn money, and in the second half, we sacrifice our money to recover health."*
> ~ Voltaire, French philosopher (1694-1778)

DO

A. Create a *positive list* of what you will do

This list should detail the actions you will take over the next two weeks in the areas of nutrition, exercise, and rhythm (100% commitment level!).

Create a **negative list** which details all the things that you would like to do without—and will do without. What decisions will you make today in the areas of nutrition, exercise, and rhythm? Take three things that you think are worthy of

---

9   Constitution of the WHO, July 22, 1946, New York

improvement and concentrate on just one. Work on this for at least two weeks—it is not about the collection of ideas, but the consistent and continuous "putting into practice." If you need ideas, you will find them in the next section of this book.

You will soon feel and see the results of what you do for your body. Enough books have been written about nutrition and so-called *stimulants,* but the recommendations we've outlined will be a natural stimulant to you as you incorporate them into your life. Take it slowly step by step; you will need to implement these changes into your daily routine, and this does not happen overnight.

B. Your task is simple but not easy

Implement this rule for two weeks. (After two weeks you can decide whether to continue with this task or go on to the next point.)

All aspects of life are interconnected and interwoven. Success and the training of the proactive muscle in the areas of nutrition, exercise, and rhythm have a direct impact on other areas of your life. With the implementation of these principles, you can achieve all that you desire: *success, power, strength, the strength of character* and *prosperity.* Now it's up to you!

C. Personal Observation (Reflection)

Choose a day in the week on which you can reflect on the events of the past week. Make it a weekly ritual; take 15 minutes and retire to a quiet place. Ask yourself: *Where did I do well in assuming responsibility and where was I reactive and not in harmony with my goals and values?* Look over the list you've made and choose one activity for next week, in which you will be more proactive. By so doing you will change your attitude week-by-week towards responsibility and personal freedom.

GROW—Immerse yourself in this principle and perform the exercises for at least two weeks. Proceed to the next lesson only if you feel confident in carrying out these exercises.

Affirmations to help you grow:

- You are making healthy choices.
- You are standing on your own two feet.
- You accept your power and strength—and make them work for you.
- It doesn't matter how others react (what they say or do) when you act based on your values.
- You respect the needs of your body.
- You eat consciously, what is good for your body.
- You take responsibility for your health. You are healthy.
- You look forward to a healthy old age since you are lovingly taking care of your body.

CHAPTER 3

GRATITUDE

BECOME THANKFUL

BE **THANKFUL** FOR WHAT YOU HAVE; YOU'LL END UP HAVING MORE. IF YOU **CONCENTRATE** ON WHAT YOU DON'T HAVE, YOU WILL NEVER, EVER HAVE ENOUGH.

OPRAH WINFREY

Like summer, being grateful is something to **look forward to or plan for. MAXIMIZE** your opportunity to express your gratitude. Doing so will result in the **feeling of abundance** as you move into harvest time.

Gratitude, symbolized by summer, is the third principle of *Live with Intent.* Summer time is when we slow down and **live in the present.** This is when we appreciate the **NOW**; when we recognize the blessings we enjoy and people **WE LOVE.**

Being someone who is grateful means **feeling and expressing gratitude** for the people, events, experiences, and challenges in our lives. People with an attitude of gratitude are **attractive**. They draw others into their lives. Being thankful is a **MARK OF MATURITY,** an essential leadership quality.

Gordon Green[10] grew up on a farm in Canada. While the other children played ball and went swimming after school, he and his brothers and sisters came home quickly to help on the farm. Their father, however, was able to help them understand that their work was worth it. This was particularly apparent at harvest time when the family celebrated Thanksgiving. On this day the father made them aware of their great blessings—he took stock of everything they had.

On Thanksgiving morning, he took them into the cellar and showed them the barrels of apples, containers with beets, carrots covered with sand, mountains of sacks of potatoes and shelves with tins of peas, corn, green beans, jam, strawberries and other canned goods. He let the children count everything carefully, so they could see how much was there. After they were done, he took them out to the barn and had them estimate how many tons of hay were stored there and how many bushels of grain were in the granary. Next, they counted the cows, pigs, chickens, turkeys, and geese. The father said that he wanted to review the state of things, but they knew that he wanted them to be aware of how richly God blessed their family and how he had rewarded their many hours of work. When they finally sat down to the feast that their mother had prepared, only then could they really feel how blessed they were.

Green did, however, point out that he remembered, with the utmost gratitude, a year in which it seemed as if they had nothing for which they might be grateful.

The year began well: They had hay from last year, a lot of seed, four litters of piglets and their father had put a little money aside for a hay loader—a wonderful machine that most farmers dreamed of having. That year their town was also connected to the electricity grid, but their farm was not connected because they could not afford it.

One night when Mother Green was washing clothes, her husband came in, took over the washboard and told his wife to go rest. He said: "You spend more time washing than sleeping. Do you think we should lay electricity cables?" Despite the

---

10   Gordon Green, H., *The Thanksgiving I Don't Forget*, Reader's Digest, November 1956, p. 69ff.

positive outlook, she shed tears when she thought of not buying the hay loader.

So that year, for the first time, they had electric light. They bought a simple washing machine that worked all day by itself and had light bulbs dangling from the ceiling in every room. Now they no longer had to fill the lamps with oil, cut wicks, or clean sooty fireplaces. The oil lamps were stowed away in the attic without much fuss.

The power connection for their farm was about the last good thing to happen that year. When the seeds started to sprout, it started to rain hard, washing away all the plants. They planted again, but again the rain drowned the seed. The potatoes rotted in the mud. Only a few turnips and beets survived the storm. Desperate for cash, they sold a couple of cows and all the pigs and other livestock that they wanted to keep, but they received very low prices because everyone else had to do the same. When Thanksgiving came, the mother said, "It would be better to forget this year, we do not even have a goose left over."

On the morning of Thanksgiving, Father Green appeared with a rabbit and asked his wife to prepare it for dinner. Reluctantly, she went to work, as the tough old rabbit had to be cooked for a long time. When the roast rabbit was finally served with a few beets, the children refused to eat it, and Mother Green wept. The father then went up to the attic, got an oil lamp, placed it on the table and lit it. He asked the children to turn off the electric light, as the room was only lit by the lamp. They could hardly believe that the room was so dark. They wondered how they had ever seen anything without the bright electric light.

The blessing on the food was said, and everyone ate. After dinner, they all sat still. Green wrote: "In the dim light of the old oil lamps we suddenly saw very clearly. It was a good meal. The rabbit tasted like a turkey, and the beets were the best that we had ever tasted. Even though there was so little there, we felt extremely rich."

Feeling and Expressing Gratitude

Gratitude is one of the noblest moral virtues. It connects us to the world and with other people in a peaceful manner. It is good to develop a grateful attitude towards life because thankful people are at peace and content with themselves.

Somebody who takes a balanced assessment of the day, every evening, for example by writing in his diary and asking "What am I thankful for today?" or "What happened today that I am grateful for?" will be less egocentric and proud—and more responsible for his own actions—and not pass the blame. Selfish love revolves around thinking only of ourselves and taking pride only in our achievements; it separates us from the company of others and turns us into cold individuals.

Gratitude binds us to others in respect. It allows us to warm to each other and brings us a mutual appreciation for our lives and deeds. When we receive something that can't be returned in kind or compensated, gratitude is the only thing that helps. Bernd Hellinger, a systemic family therapist, says: "Gratitude is the great leveling out!"

Beyond expressing gratitude for the good people and things in our lives, we also need to consider the good that can come from adversity—from tough conditions, bad situations, and experiences that cause us pain. Rather than remain in sadness, denial or self-pity, we might ask:

Why should I feel grateful for this life experience?
Who should I thank for this experience?
What can I learn from this situation?

By asking such questions, we see that even our unpleasant, serious or tragic circumstances can be beneficial because these life struggles end with our own destiny. As we look closely, we see that the biggest challenges, the enormous struggles of our life can become our strongest resources over time. This truth is hard to accept when we are in the situation; however, you and I do have a choice. You can be thankful for all you are receiving, even if it is hard right now.

The first requirement is to recognize the *here and now* as the fertile starting point of our own development and accept it as such. We can look at our situations and options in a new light when we take stock of our lives and the abilities that we possess and consider the debt of gratitude we owe to good people for their positive influence in our lives.

Yes, egotism, selfishness, greed, pleasure-seeking, cruelty, and crimes ruin many lives; but we can rebuild our lives by breaking free from negative thought patterns and by cultivating an attitude of gratitude in our hearts. When the noble virtue of gratitude is applied daily in our actions and speech, it uplifts and protects us; ingratitude only burdens us.

Good Example: Patrick Pichette

Layoffs in business are usually very negatively charged events, and letters of gratitude are rarely written by those who are terminated.

In March 2015 Larry Page, co-founder of Google, shared the resignation of his Chief Financial Officer (CFO) *Patrick Pichette* on the social network site Google Plus. He wrote that it was a highly unusual termination of an unusual CFO; the letter is very worth reading because it is very heart-warming. [11] Here is Patrick's entire farewell letter:

After nearly 7 years as CFO, I will be retiring from Google to spend more time with my family. Yeah, I know you've heard that line before. We give a lot to our jobs. I certainly did. And while I am not looking for sympathy, I want to share my thought process because so many people struggle to strike the right balance between work and personal life.

This story starts last fall. A very early morning last September, after a whole night of climbing, looking at the sunrise on top of Africa—Mt Kilimanjaro. Tamar (my wife) and I were not only enjoying the summit, but on such a clear day, we could see in the distance the vast plain of the Serengeti at our feet, and with it the calling of all the potential adventures Africa has to offer. And Tamar out of the blue said, "Hey, why don't we just keep on going? Let's explore Africa, and then turn east to make our way to India, it's just next door, and we're here already. Then, we keep going; the

---

11   See Page Larry on the Google plus platform on March 10, 2015, https://plus. google.com/+LarryPage/posts/THXDPTgTFcb, accessed on 08/27/2015

Himalayas, Everest, go to Bali, the Great Barrier Reef... Antarctica, let's go see Antarctica!?" Little did she know, she was tempting fate.

I remember telling Tamar a typical prudent CFO type response, "I would love to keep going, but we have to go back. It's not time yet. There is still so much to do at Google, with my career, so many people counting on me/us –boards, non-profits, etc."

But then she asked the killer question: "So when is it going to be time? Our time? My time?" The questions just hung there in the cold morning African air.

A few weeks later, I was happy back at work but could not shake away THE question: When is it time for us to just keep going? And so began a reflection on my/our life. Through numerous hours of cycling last fall (my introvert happy place) I concluded on a few simple and self-evident truths:

First, the kids are gone. Two are in college, one graduated and the other one in a start-up in Africa. Beautiful young adults we are very proud of. Tamar honestly deserves most of the credit here. She has done a marvelous job. Simply marvelous. But the reality is that for Tamar and I, there will be no more Cheerios-encrusted minivan, night watch because of ear infections, ice hockey rinks at 6 a.m. Nobody is waiting for us/needing us.

Second, I am completing this summer 25-30 years of nearly non-stop work (depending on how you wish to cut the data). And being a member of FWIO, the noble Fraternity of Worldwide Insecure Over-achievers, it has been a whirlwind of truly amazing experiences. But as I count it now, it has also been a frenetic pace for about 1,500 weeks now. Always on—even when I was not supposed to be. Especially when I was not supposed to be. And am guilty as charged—I love my job (still do), my colleagues, my friends, the opportunities to lead and change the world.

Third, this summer, Tamar and I will be celebrating our 25th anniversary. When our kids are asked by their friends about the success of the longevity of our marriage, they simply joke that Tamar and I have spent so little time together that "it's really too early to tell" if our marriage will in fact succeed. If they only knew how many great memories we already have together. How many will you say? How long do you have? But one thing is for sure, I want more. And she deserves more. Lots more.

Allow me to spare you the rest of the truths. But the short answer is simply that I could not find a good argument to tell Tamar we should wait any longer for us to grab our backpacks and hit the road—celebrate our last 25 years together by turning the page and enjoy a perfectly fine mid-life crisis full of bliss and beauty, and leave the door open to serendipity for our next leadership opportunities, once our long list of travels and adventures is exhausted.

Working at Google is a privilege, nothing less. I have worked with the best of the best, and know that I am leaving Google in great hands. I have made so many friends at Google it's not funny. Larry, Sergey, Eric, thank you for your friendship. I am forever grateful for letting me be me, for your trust, your warmth, your support, and for so much laughter through good and not so good times.

To be clear, I am still here. I wish to transition over the coming months but only after we have found a new Google CFO and help him/her through an orderly transition, which will take some time.

In the end, life is wonderful, but nonetheless a series of trade-offs, especially between business/professional endeavors and family/community. And thankfully, I feel I'm at a point in my life where I no longer have to have to make such tough choices anymore. And for that I am truly grateful. Carpe Diem.-Patrick[12]

Thomas: This ode to the company and to his family is a remarkable letter. In it, Patrick Pichette shows gratitude towards his employer and his family. By showing the virtue of gratitude in action, he enabled a gentle, even inspiring exit—one filled with mutual respect. Let's look deeper as to how to apply the virtue of gratitude in our personal lives.

---

12   Page Larry on the Google plus platform on March 10, 2015, https://plus.
google.com/+LarryPage/posts/THXDPTgTFcb, accessed on 08/27/2015

For Whom Might You Be Grateful?

You might be grateful for many people, places and things. Here are seven possible items:

Be grateful for your mother. "As long as you have a mother, thank God and be satisfied; not everyone on this earth is that fortunate"[13] or "A mother's work is the pride of the world."[14] Motherhood requires much hardship and self-sacrifice. The seemingly tireless giving of service to the needy child seems limitless and is not simply a product of hormones or a reaction to the "kiddie trend." We can never repay this active love. We can only try to compensate this selfless love by showing

---

13   Friedrich Wilhelm Kaulisch, 1827–1881

14   Maxim Gorki, 1868–1936

gratitude and appreciation to our mothers and by passing this gift onto our children. Mothers deserve, without reservation, the full gratitude of their children.

Be grateful for your father. My father, for example, was prepared to sacrifice his personal expectations for his children. Day after day he worked hard for a living without any complaints. He was and still is today completely concerned for the welfare of his family. This love for children and the desire for their well-being and happiness is a constant amid changing times. Fathers deserve, without reservation, the full gratitude of their children.

Be grateful for good teachers. Teachers shape the expectations and aspirations of their students and affect their attitude towards the future and themselves. If teachers love their students and have high expectations of them, they'll grow in confidence and create their future.

Be grateful for your spouse/partner and don't take him/her for granted. Ironically because our partner is always there and always does his/her jobs or makes openly an important contribution to our lives, we tend to regard the person as undeserving of thanks. In fact, the opposite is true: *because* he/she "always" does it and is "always" there, we should be especially grateful and appreciate and respect him/her. Our relationships and marriages are so much better when we express our gratitude for our wife or husband in a kind and respectful manner, regularly! Be careful what you want—you need to like the consequences of what you want. So, be grateful! Cherish what is. *What is* could be the highlight of your life.

Be grateful for your children and family. Regardless of how much work, effort and worry your children give you, treasure the precious moments that you experience with them. Be grateful for their existence—you will live on through them. And be grateful for your family; cultivate deep connections and meaningful relationships with them.

Be grateful for your friends. True friends accept our idiosyncrasies and greatly bless our lives. Your friends and professional colleagues are among the greatest treasures in your life.

Be grateful for your country and your home. Remember the personal price that your ancestors and others paid for your freedom. Many paid that price with their lives; others lost their husbands or fathers, brothers or friends. Acknowledge that you enjoy tremendous dividends from their contributions.

Grateful people see many positives in the world. For them, good triumphs over evil; love conquers jealousy; and light chases out darkness. Pride and arrogance destroy gratitude and replace it with selfishness. Are we not happier when we are in the presence of a thankful and positive person? Don't wait until it is too late to express your gratitude. When we lose a loved one, we often regret that we did not express more often our gratitude for them. So, express your love and gratitude regularly to your loved ones. You never know when it will be too late!

Show Appreciation: Cultivate a Grateful Heart

We tend to separate our experiences into categories such as right and wrong, good and bad. The more we prejudge people and places, the more we limit ourselves in having genuine new experiences. Moreover, an over-dependence on material things can limit our happiness. Many people take their identity from their material possessions.

Genuine appreciation begins with you. Appreciate yourself and your life. Have compassion for yourself when things don't go as planned or when you experience setbacks. Speak positively and lovingly to yourself. Watch your self-talk, and silence your inner critic.

Too often we rely on the estimation of those around us, which makes us dependent upon the opinion and appreciation of others. Fritz Pearls, the founder of Gestalt therapy, said: "*If you need praise and pats on the back, then you invite everyone to be your judge.*"

Dare to have and apply your own opinion about life—then your life will have enormous power and value. Allow yourself to bring out the best in yourself.

> "*The increase of luxury: own apartment,*
> *own auto, own opinion.*"
> ~ *Wieslaw Brudzunski*

Have you realized that when you try to get appreciation from outside sources, you often don't receive it? However, if you value yourself, you will, step by step, be able to influence everything in your environment.

How do you show appreciation to other people?
- Keep away from prejudice and pride—walls through which appreciation cannot break.
- Strive to understand those around you with compassion.
- Show others respect, regardless of who it is and where he or she is coming from.

How do you show yourself honest, authentic appreciation?
- No matter the direction your life goes, stay true to your dreams, your goals and your beliefs—don't give up on them.
- Don't judge yourself—regardless of your situation.
- No one does it better in your situation than you.
- If you are dissatisfied with your life, energize yourself and change it!
- Become aware of what is not good for you, and discuss with those around you what you do not like. Make changes that everyone can live with. Life is too short to make unconscious compromises or just "endure."

TIP

SEE—Write spontaneously to whom or for what you are grateful:

Now, think about past situations that were involuntary disruptions in your life. Look at them closely and SEE from today's standpoint what you have learned from these situations and what you are thankful for. Jot down a few key points in your learning diary. As you review your past, ask: To whom do you still owe a debt of gratitude? You may think of someone to whom you are indebted and owe a "thank you." Perhaps you think that it is too long ago, and the chance has gone? Don't let that thought stop you—finish your unfinished business. It doesn't matter if the recipient of your gratitude is still living or not.

What small things can you express gratitude for—even small things that you consider to be unimportant and tend to disregard? Perhaps the bus driver who opens the door when you get to the bus late, or the woman at the cash register who carefully checks every item across the conveyor belt? Take note of people to whom you want to give recognition or express appreciation. Do it now!

DO

A. Ten miracles along the way—four beans

Gratitude requires awareness and perception. By finding ways to regularly be aware of this, you will feel an inner confirmation that will bring you great joy even in small things. Look for 10 miracles that you have experienced today. Write them in your learning diary. I always carry four beans in my trouser pocket. When I see something for which I am grateful, I transfer one bean from the left pocket into the right pocket. In so doing I can be sure at the end of the day that I have paid enough attention to those things for which I am grateful. Try it!

B. Reflection

How do you feel when someone expresses gratitude to you?
How do you feel when you say "thank you" to someone?

C. Gifts

When we have gratitude in our hearts, we are prompted
to thank those around us for all that they enrich our lives
with. This requires a great deal of effort until this attitude is
ingrained in our bodies and souls. We often feel grateful for
things and intend to express that gratitude, but then we forget
to say it or don't get around to saying it. "To feel gratitude and
then not to express it is like wrapping up a present and then not
giving it[15]." Which gift have you not given?

D. Gratitude in difficult situations

During difficult times of tribulation, find reasons to be
grateful. You and your heart will increase and grow, and people
around you will be aware of your change. A grateful heart
brings forth the coveted fruit of inner peace. This is what other
people will see and feel in your presence.

E. Self-appreciation

Are you in a situation in which you are not satisfied? What
do you have to change in your life to feel more satisfied? Adopt
the attitude of considering it unacceptable to remain in an
unsatisfactory situation. Do you have such situations in your
life? If so, which ones?

GROW—The following affirmations and checklist will help
you as you grow in appreciation.

Affirmations
- You receive valuable gifts from life every day.
- It will all work out for the good.
- You have the strength to change things that no longer
  conform to your life.

---

15   William Arthur Ward, quoted in: *Change Your Life!*, Ed. Allen Klein, 2010,
     p. 15

- Your biggest challenges are your biggest resources.

Work on this chapter for two weeks before moving on to the next one.

Checklist

1. Even the smallest act of friendship is not a matter of course.
2. Cultivate humility in yourself.
3. Learn to accept wholehearted compliments and acts of friendship.
4. Be thankful for your life experiences and for the benevolence of your family, your partner and your friends, who helped make you the person you now are.
5. Believe in yourself and in your skills.
6. Work on your strengths—they are the keys to personal growth. Everything except fatal flaws can be compensated for by developing your strengths.

CHAPTER 4
SELF-CONFIDENCE

BE AT PEACE WITHIN YOURSELF

IF **I AM WHAT I HAVE**, AND WHAT I HAVE IS LOST, **WHO THEN AM I?**

ERICH FROMM

Self-Confidence, symbolized by fall, is the fourth principle of *Live with Intent*. Fall time is when we harvest. An abundant harvest brings a feeling of **PEACE**, **SECURITY**, and **CONFIDENCE** in our ability to provide for ourselves and others.

Being **self-confident** means being at peace with who we are and what we **CONTRIBUTE**; feeling the fruits of our labor and recognizing the difference we have made in the world around us; and celebrating our efforts and accomplishments.

As in nature, after the harvest and before winter we can **LET GO** of anything and everything that is stealing our peace. Doing so **will prepare you** for turning inward and building up your **RESERVES** throughout the winter.

One **CORE** social problem of our day concerns the lack of **self-esteem.**

Insecurity and a shallow self-image may be related to building **our identities** upon what we have, instead of who we are.

Since humility and **GENTLENESS** too often do not readily trade in the marketplace, some may think that they can live by whatever standards they feel like. Living **FREE of personal standards** can leave you living free of a feeling of **self-worth, self-respect and self-confidence.**

Our own integrity towards the values we stand for is a substantial part of our individual **WORTH** and self-confidence. Can we **respect ourselves** when we do things that we do not admire and may even condemn in others?

Justin: On July 12, 1986, at age 18, I discovered who I had become. Riding down the Sundance Canyon in Utah with my girlfriend, I was shouting at her, treating her like no human being should ever be treated. She eventually broke down in tears and drove me back to the Sundance Resort, where I was scheduled to serve dinner to the resort's owner and his guests at his private residence.

The episode started as I was walking across the Sundance parking lot on my way to work. She pulled up in her car and said, "Jump in for a minute. I have a question for you." As soon as I sat down, she popped the clutch and sped away. I wondered, what is she thinking? She knew I was scheduled at the owner's private home that day. Girlfriend or not, nothing was going to get in the way of my reputation as the top dog with the privileged assignments.

As we pulled back into the parking lot that day, a large group of people had assembled on the front lawn. I first saw the balloons and then noticed the buffet tables lined with kitchen equipment. Full of myself, I further justified my anger. How could she do this to me? Now I was late to work and the best equipment had probably been used for the pleasant picnic on the lawn. I needed the equipment for the owner's party.

She conceded defeat and dropped me off in front of the restaurant. As I slammed the car door and stormed away, I saw two friends from high school who greeted me with "happy birthday." In that moment, the revelation came to me with bomb-like force: there was no party at the owner's private residence; the party on the front lawn was for me. My girlfriend had colluded with my boss to use the "private" event as a decoy to ensure I would make it to my own party—a party she had spent weeks preparing for and ensuring everyone I knew would attend.

Everyone was there—from high school, from Sundance, everyone in my life. Everyone was there to witness my failed behavior.

My surprise and joy were overshadowed by shame and deep embarrassment. My character had been revealed. My values had been revealed. Anything but humble or gentle, I had literally beat down the very person who was trying to celebrate my life.

For weeks, sadness and shame haunted me, humbled me. I had become a proud, selfish and even vulgar person. What happened? How had I become what I despised in others?

My identity had become tangled up in my position and sense of success at work. I had lost track of my personal standards, and as a result, found myself humiliated, lacking feelings of self-confidence, self-worth and dignity.

Somewhere in my shame and suffering I made a promise to myself. From my soul I promised I would never again treat another human being like I had treated her. Never again would I allow work to be more important than people.

Looking back over the past 20 years, it is interesting to observe how I have become gentler with myself and others. I have spent most of my adult life helping other people discover who they are, what matters most to them and why their lives matter.

I have learned that self-confidence comes from a deep belief in who we are, not in what we have. We all make mistakes, have setbacks and discover our own character flaws. Our experiences with failure can lead us to a greater understanding of who we are, what talents we have and why we matter. I have experienced how overcoming a weakness is a great restorative salve for strengthening self-worth, self-confidence and dignity.

I have learned that empowering your self-confidence brings peace.

"Serenity is a lovely woman and lives amongst wisdom."
~ Epicharm (circa 540 BC)

Thomas: Empower Your Self-Confidence. *True strength comes from calmness.* This is a principle of great importance. It affects not only how you see the world but also your physical abilities and general well-being. The influence that you have over others is different when you are at peace with yourself and "self-aware".

Conversely, think about a man who is motivated by agitation, bustle and nervousness. Would we attribute to him a high level of expertise, power, security and strength? Certainly not.

We will begin slowly and carefully using our existing energy and strength and then develop our newfound strengths. We tend to assume that our daily tasks and jobs rob us of our strength and energy, and that we have private time to replenish our batteries. We assume that an intensive day of work saps our energy and strength and increases our stress. However, work done with passion and zeal can actually add positive stress (*eustress*), which is not exhausting. Stress results more from the build-up of little things that have a negative impact on us and leaves us tired (*distress*): trouble with clients or colleagues; customer complaints that could have been avoided; annoying mistakes; or the bad mood of a boss or colleague. When you are hit by this negative wave, you naturally feel such negative emotions as fear, anger, or anxiety.

Exhaustion is different from fatigue. Fatigue may derive from the feeling of a job well done; in contrast, exhaustion often derives from the feeling of what was *not* done.

Small Excursion into Exhaustion

In alternative medicine a common expression is *"Fatigue is the cry of pain from the liver."* What does that mean? In contrast to other vital organs—such as the kidney, gall bladder, stomach, and heart—the liver does not give an indication of its pain.

However, *discomfort* expresses itself in *fatigue*. The liver regulates detoxification. If the metabolic end products have an acidic nature and gain the upper hand, the liver is overworked; since the body is not adequately detoxified, fatigue sets in. And if fatigue continues, regeneration (the second major responsibility of the liver) is severely impaired. On the one hand, overdoing things tires us; on the other hand, we are tired by doing too little. We may suffer from exhaustion simply because we have not accomplished an important assignment.

Composure

Imagine being in a situation where you would like to be composed, and yet you feel nervous. For example:

- After making a sales presentation, a colleague, Jim, makes fun of you in front of the whole team; you are so surprised and embarrassed that you can't say anything.
- While reading the newspaper, you discover that stock market prices have again fallen, which concerns you greatly and causes your forehead to crease into frowns.
- On the way home, you meet Ken, who is not your greatest fan. You feel his ironic and judgmental attitude washing over you and your heart starts to beat faster!

If you study these three examples, you can see that these kinds of daily irritations should not derail you; and yet they may agitate you, make you nervous, or even give you an inferiority complex. You would like to be composed, and yet you discover that composure is not easy to achieve. How can you be calm in such situations? Perhaps you get up in the morning intent on not getting angry or becoming stressed, but by noon your peace of mind has been destroyed.

Composure is not a matter of your conscious will. It does not help to make energetic decisions to clench your fists and convince yourself to not be upset. There will always be days when your emotions are stronger than your intentions, and if we work on our challenges only by putting more pressure on ourselves, personal failure will hit even harder.

But how can you strengthen your composure and cope better with frustrations? The answer lies in using your breathing as a key to your composure. We suggest doing simple *breathing exercises throughout the day*. Be intentional about your breathing on your way to work, in meetings, in difficult or important situations.

Your physical condition and peace of mind are intertwined. For example, by acting cheerful and happy, you actually become happy! Or, by trying to make a child laugh, you suddenly become more light-hearted and carefree. Each emotion has a direct effect on your breathing. If you are frightened, you instinctively hold your breath; when you realize that the danger is over, you let out a huge sigh of relief.

Laughing, crying, coughing, clearing your throat and sighing are all direct expressions of the soul, as well as various forms of breathing. Trembling hands or blushing suddenly will also impact your breathing rhythm. As long as you can breathe calmly and evenly, your trembling hands, blushing or other outward signs of emotion are held in check.

Training and guiding your breathing is highly valued in Yoga[16] as it has a calming and purging effect on your inner spirit. The faster an animal breathes, the lower its life expectancy (compare the mouse with the tortoise).

You can consciously adjust the speed of your breathing with this exercise: Take a short walk. Move *briskly and evenly*, perhaps using walking sticks. Avoid conversation. Count how many steps you take as you breathe in. You might take four or five steps or more before you breathe out; then breathe out and count how many steps you take until you take your next breath. It should be the same amount of steps for breathing in and breathing out. Continue counting and walking for another 15 minutes. With practice you'll gain more breathing volume, and soon you'll feel calm and comfortable. Adrenaline, the hormone secreted when you are angry or stressed (enabling you to take flight), is diverted into a soothing motion. Therefore, it has no further damaging effect on your body. You become inaccessible to anger and stress. Even the careless driver who almost hits your car cannot upset you. This wonderful feeling usually continues for some time.

In times of severe stress, you should repeat this breathing exercise several times during the day. Soon the effects will become evident. The higher your tension, the more you should march! Gradually your breathing volume will increase, and you will take more steps between taking breathes. Practice this exercise regularly, with concentration, until it becomes indelibly imprinted in your body and becomes an automatic procedure. Obviously, don't practice this exercise to the point of exhaustion—it should always be carried out with ease, at an

16   Hatha Yoga

even pace and with goal-orientated determination; if so, it will result in feelings of happiness and well-being.

Shyness

Many sensitive but capable people find it difficult to be outgoing. Their shyness has nothing to do with having an inferiority complex. Rather, they may be too aware of the opinions of others. What you will learn in Chapter 8 about autosuggestion to be composed and calm will help you to overcome shyness.

If shyness is an issue for you, please follow two suggestions: 1) Since regular repetition of the deep breathing exercises can bring you calmness and composure at any time, repeat it every time you encounter difficult people or situations; 2) find and then repeat over a few weeks a suitable autosuggestion; for example: *I am calm and strong in difficult situations. My breathing is steady and gives me power. Even when facing opposition, I am calm and level-headed. With each breath I take, stress and anger are reduced.*

Repeat this exercise until you achieve a stable result. Re-do this exercise every time you encounter situations that cause you to feel insecure and reduce your self-confidence. Knowing that you are smart and suitably dressed can also give you a feeling of confidence—so you need to be well-groomed. Take care to ensure that each day you are impeccably and correctly dressed. Work on good posture and body tension. As you maintain a good external appearance, your internal feelings will match. Balancing exercises will help you to acquire a firm foundation.

Find yourself a good positive reference—one with which you feel comfortable—and repeat this in front of a mirror so that your internal confidence will reflect your external demeanor. When you are around people or in situations that intimidate you, go into that rehearsed strong stance.

In our muscles are small receptors that report the actual state of our brain. A slumped posture, a sullen or sad face are reported to the brain, as is an upright posture and smiling facial expression. And the corresponding emotions are perceived and sent out.

You need to have a *spirit of excellence* and maintain a confident attitude, especially when you are alone or with people who do not intimidate you, such as your friends or your family. By doing this, a positive, confident attitude will become second nature to you.

Do not think about or dwell on your weaknesses! Think of something that you are good at or that makes you happy! Focus solely on what you have to say and do. Quietly give yourself the corresponding *autosuggestion*. For example: *I am calm and strong, I am in control* etc.

One entrepreneur who has internalized this is Elon Musk. In 2015, the American business journalist Ashlee Vance published his biography entitled *Elon Musk: Tesla, SpaceX, and the Quest for a Fantastic Future.*[17] Vance's central thesis is: "This Musk is unstoppable. The Tesla-maker is not interested in what others think about him or whether there is resistance. He has goals that he wants to achieve, no matter what it costs. The man will not stop." If things go wrong, Musk simply goes on. Tesla has often stood on the brink of extinction. But even in dire setbacks Musk doesn't give way, but starts again from the beginning."[18] Elon Musk is one of the most exciting personalities of the 21st century and is already being compared with Thomas Edison and Steve Jobs[19] by making the impossible possible with almost infinite confidence.

His story begins with the sale of the online payment service PayPal to eBay, for which he received $165 million in

---

17   See Weddeling, B., *Das Erfolgsgeheimnis von Elon Musk*, http://www.handelsblatt.com/unternehmen/management/biografie-des-tesla-chefs-das-serfolgegeheimnis-von-elon-musk/11798852.html, published on 05/20/2015, accessed on 08/31/2015

18   Weddeling, B., *Das Erfolgsgeheimnis von Elon Musk*, http://www.handelsblatt.com/unternehmen/management/biografie-des-tesla-chefs-das-beginn-gold-museum/11798852.html, published on 05/20/2015, accessed on 08/31/2015

19   See Worall, S., *Elon Musk, A man of impossible dreams, wants to colonize Mars*, in National Geographic, http://news.nationalgeographic.com/2015/06/150628-tesla-paypal-elon-musk-technology-steve- Jobs-silicon-valley-electric-car-ngbooktalk/, published on 06/28/2015, accessed on 08/31/2015

2002. He invested $70 million in the company SpaceX, which aims to carry out manned missions to Mars. He invested another $30 million in Solar City, which manufactures solar modules which will revolutionize power generation as well as consumption. Another $70 million he invested in the carmaker Tesla[20], which could rewrite the future of cars by electrical rather than the usual combustion engines. "Tesla is more than a car manufacturer—it is a technology and design company that is committed to innovative energy solutions."[21] This is the challenge on the company's website.

Elon Musk pursues his goals consistently. His self-confidence, his composure and his deep belief in his vision drove him almost to bankruptcy.[22] The belief in his objectives has not left Elon Musk in the lurch—he now has assets estimated at $10 billion.[23]

---

20 Guldner, J., *Keine Pause, kein Urlaub, kein Essen – nur Arbeit*, in www. zeit.de,   http://www.zeit.de/wirtschaft/2015-05/tesla-elon-musk-spacex, publication on 20.05 .2015, accessed on 08/31/2015

21 www.tesla.de, Über Tesla, http://www.teslamotors.com/de_DE/about, accessed on 08/31/2015

22 See Davies, A., *How Elon Musk is revolutionizing two major industries at the same time*, http://www.businessinsider.com/how-elon-musk-overcomes-challenges-2013-3?IR=T, published on 03/13/2013, accessed on 08/31/2015

23 See Worall, S., *Elon Musk, A man of impossible dreams, wants to colonize Mars*, in National Geographic, http://news.nationalgeographic. com/2015/06/150628-tesla-paypal-elon-musk-technology-steve-Jobs-silicon-valley-electric-car-ngbooktalk/, published on 06/28/2015, accessed on 08/31/2015

TIP

SEE—Are you at peace with yourself? If not, what would it take for you to be at peace? How would your life be different? How would your life feel different? In the end, all roads to self-confidence go through establishing peace with yourself, with who you are, with what you stand for as well as the value you create for others.

In Part 2 of this book, we will explore the exciting topic of where you are going next. For now, it is essential for you to see where you are now in terms of being at peace with yourself.

Once you are at peace with yourself, move on to the next chapter. Until then, take the time to make whatever corrections are necessary. Essential to getting to where you want to go is to be at peace with yourself.

Three questions may be useful in understanding what is holding back your self-confidence:
- Am I behaving in a way that is contrary to the standards I have set for myself?
- Are there any misdeeds in my life that have not been resolved?
- Am I sharing my gifts and talents to the best of my ability?

DO—The following techniques will help you stay at peace as you face the daily stresses and pressures of life. They will help you show up in life with confidence and composure.

A. Breathing exercises
Perform the breathing exercises regularly twice a day for 20 minutes—especially when facing a high degree of anger and adversity or feeling a high level of excitement.

B. Composure
Make a list of people who intimidate you and who you have previously avoided; now try actively to meet these people.

Start with the ones who fluster you the least, then move on to the ones who throw you off balance. Make yourself aware of what you're afraid of—what the worst thing that could happen might be. Often unconscious fears are exaggerated beyond what could actually happen. Realistically examining the worst-case scenario can help temper those fears.

By giving our fear a name, it becomes tangible; thus, the horror usually loses its power. Just like we call hurricanes and storms by name. The more we understand and face our fears, the more likely we are to overcome them. Realize that the person who is opposite you has also worn nappies, overcome a first kiss and had to endure exam stress. He needs to go to the toilet like any other human being and feels hunger and disappointment just like you.

By really visualizing the person to be a human being like you, you practice little by little to feel relaxed and confident in the presence of others.

It is virtually the same procedure with making telephone calls. Please be aware that although the person on the other end of the line can't see you, he or she can still hear you well. Assume an upright posture, even though the person cannot see you. Often it helps to stand upright during a call. Move your lips as if you were trying to annunciate very clearly. What you probably find funny will come across as clear and articulate to the person at the other end of the line.

If you find yourself consistently procrastinating certain types of phone calls or discussions, schedule time each week to focus on these interactions. With the conviction that comes from autosuggestion and breathing exercises, you can maintain the mental picture of how you will feel after you complete the task. As you practice, you will begin to feel a sense of power and achievement.

Take things slowly at first. Don't worry if you do not see immediate progress. The important thing is not to feel pressured. Your time will come!

GROW—These **affirmations** will help you accelerate your growth.
- You are at peace with yourself; all good things are coming together.
- You are perfectly okay just as you are.
- Everything in your life turns out for the better.
- You're okay; they're okay; he's okay; she's okay.

This **checklist** provides ideas for building momentum as you grow your self-confidence.
- Do a specific slow-down. Stress, hustle and bustle and nervousness hinder your productivity and limit your effectiveness.
- Avoid being influenced by negative changes or small annoyances. You can't change the past, but you can change the sources of your power.
- Do your breathing exercises.
- Work with your shyness through autosuggestion.
- Work in an upright and confident posture.
- Always dress appropriately for the situation.
- In stressful and unpleasant situations, focus on your strengths.
- Continue the breathing exercises as you study this book.

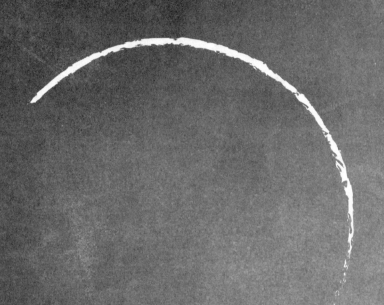

Part 2

Where You Are Going

WHERE YOU ARE GOING

CONNECT WITH YOUR HORIZON

In this second section, we explore the question "Where are you going?" and introduce four foundational principles: planning, visualizing, creating reality and programming our mind.

CHAPTER 5

Your Plan: Achieve meaningful goals

CHAPTER 6

Visualization: Shape your future

CHAPTER 7

Language Creates Reality: Inspire people

CHAPTER 8

Autosuggestion: Tap into fresh power

CHAPTER 5
YOUR PLAN

ACHIEVE MEANINGFUL GOALS

SO IT IS – THE LIFE WE RECEIVE IS NOT SHORT, BUT WE MAKE IT SO, NOR DO WE HAVE ANY LACK OF IT, BUT ARE WASTEFUL OF IT.

THERE ARE ONLY A FEW WHO COMMIT THEM-SELVES AND THEIR **AC-TIVITIES** TO A SOLID PLAN; THOSE REMAINING DO NOT FORGE AHEAD BUT DRIFT AWAY **LIKE A PIECE OF WOOD** THAT FLOATS ON THE WATER.

SENECA SNR. ROMAN ORA-TOR AND WRITER (CIRCA 4 BC)

Objects that take up space and have mass are called **MATTER**. **Everything around you** is made up of matter.

Matter has four states: **solid, liquid, gas and plasma.**

Part 2 of *Live with Intent* has four principles symbolized by the four states of matter. These four principles will guide you through defining **where YOU are going.**

Principle 5, **YOUR PLAN**, is symbolized by the solid state. A **solid plan** feels concrete and gives you a sense of **STABILITY**.

Your Plan is about making solid, meaningful **GOALS**. Once your goals are **CONCRETE**, we will use three additional principles of **visualization, language and autosuggestion** that will help you move through the next three states.

Thomas: Be intentional about how you use your time in making a meaningful contribution; have a plan for creating the type of legacy you wish to leave behind.

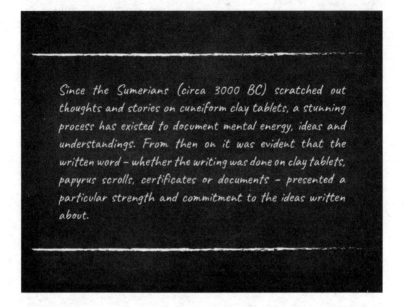

Since the Sumerians (circa 3000 BC) scratched out thoughts and stories on cuneiform clay tablets, a stunning process has existed to document mental energy, ideas and understandings. From then on it was evident that the written word – whether the writing was done on clay tablets, papyrus scrolls, certificates or documents – presented a particular strength and commitment to the ideas written about.

Harnessing the special power of the written word for your own personal purposes will enable you to make systematic progress.

Daily we encounter intelligent, hard-working people who do not live up to their potential. They may think that they cannot achieve more, or believe that fate did not deal with them kindly or that they lacked opportunity to develop themselves properly. Rather than complain or accept it, they should ask themselves: *Who directs your destiny—should it just be left to chance?*

On close examination, we see that few people ever have their life goals clearly in mind; fewer yet formulate their goals in writing. And yet having a clear view of the desired results to be achieved is one of the most decisive factors in accomplishing your goals.

Many students and high school dropouts can't decide on a profession. They don't know what might please them and what training they should undertake. Since apprenticeships are now scarce, they often have no choice but to take the next best training scheme. Even the choice of university studies sometimes does not correspond to their inner desire or goal.

At work, we see some people who are neither lazy nor stupid; yet after 10 years with the same company, they are still sitting behind the same desk earning about the same wage. When they then compare themselves with former classmates who were less intelligent but are now wealthy and fulfilled, we might as well ask, "What has happened here?"

These people failed to apply sound principles.

Many examples, like the following from IBM, prove that there is another way:

Former IBM CEO Sam Palmisano, whom the *Harvard Business Review* would be pleased to award a Nobel Prize[24], shows impressively the power of a systematic life that is standard in a business context. From 2002 to 2011, he led IBM to financial records and transformed the company into the biggest IT enterprise in the world.[25]

How did he manage that? His success was motivated by his willingness to win the biggest stakeholders over to his company. And he had a "model" (we could also call it a *plan*). This model contained a road map for the next several years, with respect to earnings growth and liquid resources.[26] Sam's model can be split into four parts:

1. *Strategy*: Here, he defines the future divisions in which the business generates revenues.

---

24   See Bower, J.L., *Sam Palmisano's Transformation of IBM*, in Harvard Business Review, January 20, 2012, https://hbr.org/2012/01/sam-palmisanos-transformation, accessed on 10/16/2015

25   See Harvard Business Manager, *Harvard discussions. Top managers in the interview: What you can learn from the big ones*, in Edition 3/2015, accessed on 08/25/2015

26   See Harvard Business Manager, *Harvard discussions. Top managers in the interview: What you can learn from the big ones*, in Edition 3/2015, accessed on 08/25/2015

2. **Budget**: Derived from the strategy, there is a financial plan that is transparently shared with the stakeholders. Transparency is a key word here.
3. **Management system**: This is derived from the budget. Each unit has to develop its own way to carry out this roadmap. When planning, it is crucial to consider that not every unit achieves perfect results—it is more realistic to call out good results as a goal.
4. **Compensation model**: The compensation model aims to reinforce the success. Employees understand that they will be rewarded when they follow the model strategy.

In this way there is a cycle in which the company's strategy pulls through like a thread from the beginning until the end.[27] With this sustained roadmap, Sam Palmisano promised an increase of the IBM stock price from $6 in 2006 to $10 in the year 2010.

The development of the model took a long time to complete. So the first version was published four years after his inauguration as the successor to CEO Lou Gerstner, and it took another period of time until the markets accepted his model. For this reason, Jim Cramer of CNBC loudly called for Sam Palmisano's resignation in 2007.

Despite the massive headwinds, Sam Palmisano remained true to his model and his principle of planning—with overwhelming success: He reached his goal of $10 per share one year early in 2009.[28] In retrospect, he says: "I learned an important lesson along the way (about the transformation of IBM): It's not easy to go to the future. You need to be confident about what you think the future holds. That said, if a business doesn't have a view about the future, it can't allocate resources to position itself to get there."[29]

---

27 See Harvard Business Review, *Managing Investors*, in June 2014 Issue, https://hbr.org/2014/06/managing-investors, accessed on 10/18/2015

28 See Harvard Business Review, *Managing Investors*, in June 2014 Issue, https://hbr.org/2014/06/managing-investors, accessed on 10/18/2015

29 The Center for Global Enterprise, *Competing in the Global Era*, p. 16, http://thecge.net/slideshare/, accessed on 10/18/2015

The process of looking ahead to the target and not sticking to the current or former status is the really inspiring part about this example from the international business world.

It is amazing to see how we plan certain events—such as a birthday party or a holiday with family or friends—with exactness and fortitude, and yet seldom think about or plan the next 365 days or the rest of our lives. Even in organizations with ample resources of time and brain power, meaningful plans and reflection cycles are often missing. This surprises some people from the outside because the benefits of planning are well-known and proven.

We are convinced that too often "potential genius" in society, business, art or literature gets lost along the way and is not discovered. This could be rectified by a person having one clear goal that could have been pursued step-by-step.

This chapter will show you how to define the goals that will help you to direct your life and help you to implement your plans.

So, How Do You Determine Your Goals?

What are your goals? Today, the most popular goal is to have a lot of money. Other popular goals are: to be famous or to stand in the limelight; to stay young-looking and to be fit; to be admired; or to have influence or power. All these goals have something in common—they are all part of a wish to be loved and to have or maintain control.

Other goals may be: to reduce the pain and misery in the world; to have a stable marriage and happy family; to generate a large circle of friends; to invent something or to otherwise bring something new into the world; or to create a solid company or to grow an existing one, or other spiritual or life goals. Setting goals might be a life-altering event.

> *"Some people are so poor, all they have is money."*
> ~ *Patrick Meagher*

Justin: We had lived in Europe for nearly 10 years when I realized that some of my long-term goals were no longer important to me. They were distracting me from doing what brought me the most satisfaction. I was sitting in the warm sun on the charming Greek island of Paros where every house is painted white with blue shutters. Peter Seibt—a fascinating man, an artist who lives life on his own terms—had invited my business partner, Martin, to his art studio overlooking the sea. Thankfully Martin had invited me. I had a life-changing event.

Mesmerized by the dark blue water contrasted against the light-blue sky, I could feel, and even taste, the salty air on my face. As we looked out over the water, Peter described the concept of constantly seeking and finding new horizons—his version of creating meaningful goals. As he talked, I tried to visualize my own goals and what I wanted from my life.

Peter started by telling us a story about nomads. He said that for thousands of years people were nomadic: Traveling light, constantly on the move toward new horizons. When nomads saw a compelling horizon—food, shelter, safety—something that made them curious, they simply packed up the tent, loaded the horses, and left.

Today, most people settle down in one place and turn their attention to accumulating possessions. When they see a new horizon—something fascinating or something they would enjoy immensely—chances are high they will not pursue it. The majority of mankind seems so busy accumulating things that their tents have become too big and their horses too few. Instead of letting go of extra baggage, traveling light and pursuing unique contributions, most people tend to stay in place, trapped by the weight of their possessions—or try in vain to bring all their things with them.

Ironically, at some point many of them end up losing their possessions anyway. They end up wishing they had ditched them years before. Wishing they had followed the horizons that offered more joy, peace and lasting satisfaction—the horizons their souls had yearned for.

Funnily enough, I went to Greece to support Martin. I had no intention of changing my life or looking for new horizons. I was satisfied with the goals I had laid out. But something changed while I was there. What changed?

I was drawn into Peter's stories about nomads, horizons, and his view of freedom. He clearly lived life on his own terms, following his own path. Swiss by birth, he chose later in life to move to a quiet island in Greece to pursue his art—to live life his own way, according to his own schedule, in his own style, independent of what other people thought.

Peter radiated a sense of peace within himself, which was attractive. His self-confidence and commitment to his unique contribution in life were, and still are, inspiring.

Five Steps to a New Horizon

Over several days, Peter led us through a simple, but profound exercise for creating a life plan based on our unique talents and wishes. Taking his *five steps* led me to my new horizon:

Step 1: Stand up. Peter illustrated how many of us still crawl around on our hands and knees. We tend to live life looking down at the ground, only seeing what is right in front of us. He literally had us moving around in the dirt outside his house on our hands and knees while asking us, with a smirk on his face, what we saw. "Dirt, weeds, ants and sticks," we responded.

"How comfortable are you?" he asked.

"Not comfortable at all," I said. "This is no fun at all."

Peter observed: "Isn't it remarkable how many of us spend life on our hands and knees, where it is uncomfortable? All we see is what is in our own little world. We are so close to the ground that we do not see what and who is around us. Now stand up and tell me what you see."

Step 2: See your horizon. We stood up and immediately the view was different: We could see the ocean and the land. The blue and brown colors, the waves, the sounds, the smells—all flooded in naturally. Stepping back and taking in the view was calming, relaxing, inspiring. There was so much more to choose from beyond the dirt, weeds, ants and sticks. We observed a vast horizon with large ships and small boats, marinas, airplanes, white sandy beaches, beautiful trees, private homes, small businesses and people moving about their day. As we gazed over the horizon, soaking in all the activity around us, Peter asked as to ponder several questions: "What fascinates you?", "What inspires you?", "Where would you like to go?", and "What would you like to discover?"

Peter challenged us to reflect on what we really wanted in life. "If you were a nomad," he asked, "what would compel you to pack up your tent, load your horses, and go?" We were instructed to visualize our next horizon on paper through art, pictures, and words.

I realized I was focused on acquiring monetary "things," like a certain type of house. I was stuck in my own little world of owning things that were not so important to me. It was like being on my hands and knees. I was uncomfortable, but believed the discomfort would eventually pay off once I reached my financial goals. I would do whatever I needed to so as to get what I wanted; what I needed. I was wrong.

My new horizon, as I visualized it, was focused less on possessions and more on experiences. I realized how important experiencing both work and play with people I enjoyed was to me. Using my talents to make a unique difference for others became a more significant part of my horizon. Combining my talents with other people to create deep relationships through doing fun, meaningful work together is what I decided to focus on. Pursuing this horizon would be living a life that mattered. A life that would make a difference for people who crossed my path.

Looking back, I realize that serving and making a difference in the lives of others was not a new horizon for me; it had already been a part of my life. However, my focus had drifted away from that path over the years. Somehow, without noticing it, I had become caught up in chasing more material things—good things, normal things, things that expressed success to people in the world around me—but things that did not fuel my spirit and make me burn for the next day. Although I was happy in life, I was unaware that I was missing something. Faint embers deep within me received oxygen that day. A fire was rekindled in my spirit; it sparked the intoxicating feeling of believing in myself; in believing that I could do *something* great with my life; that I could do something bigger and better than what I was doing; something that I could be proud of; something that my family and friends could celebrate. I knew that going forward I needed to keep this feeling burning within me and that if I could, it would give a new sense of meaning and purpose to my life. This was my renewed horizon.

This is what I still see and feel when I am on or around water. I love spending time on a boat or at the beach pondering, thinking about and expanding my horizons, feeding my spirit, visualizing my goals and documenting my life plan.

Step 3: Travel light. Our discussion emphasized the need to travel light and efficiently. "Remember the nomads," Peter said. "For thousands of years mankind was nomadic. Nomads traveled light and were constantly on the move. Today, we have created many boundaries. We have divided the world into countries, cantons, villages, private property, houses, fences, security systems—and police to protect it all. Most people have settled down and collected so much stuff; they can no longer move easily. Meanwhile globalization, financial markets, the internet and the ease of travel are evaporating these boundaries. People are increasingly on the move again."

These observations still make sense to me. I currently live in the USA, but spend 90% of my working life outside the USA. My office is 100% digital and fits in a small backpack.

Peter had each of us at his studio that week identify the vital few things that we would need to reach our next horizon. Surprisingly, in everyone's case, what we needed had more to do with our mindsets, self-beliefs and personal decisions, than with physical assets. The most important thing that I needed was a decision to be more intentional about how, and with whom, I spent my time, personally and professionally.

Step 4: Let go. Peter taught us about "ballast" and about barnacles that build up on the ships in the harbor and create drag. To demonstrate this idea, he told us the story of a woman fleeing from war. Walking across the country, burdened by her possessions, the woman looked weary and discouraged. Not knowing what the future would bring, she practically stumbled forward, with her eyes looking down at the ground. Although the weather was warm, she was dressed in several layers of clothing including a heavy fur coat—all of it clothing that she couldn't fit in the three suitcases she was half carrying, half dragging.

Each step she took was heavy. Her facial expressions clearly communicated her anger, hurt and suffering. Over the course of a few hours, the woman liberated herself. She began letting go of her things. She first parted with a suitcase. Then noticing how much easier it was with one less suitcase, she soon discarded another one as well, then the third. Then she tossed the fur coat, followed by several sweaters. In the end, she was seen walking sprightly forward with purpose, deliberate and defiant, whistling and smiling.

"How much baggage are you prepared to carry to your new horizon?", Peter asked. "What do you need to let go of if you are to reach your horizon?"

After 30 minutes of reflection, we reported back to each other what we were ready to let go of. In many cases, the things we were letting go of were possessions we desired. Things we did not even have yet! To our surprise, Peter bluntly informed us: "Your answers are superficial—you have not thought about it deeply enough. This is normal because most of us struggle to let go of our baggage." He then ended the session three hours early, told us to spend the rest of the day solo and return the next morning with a list of all the baggage we needed to discard in order to reach our desired horizon.

The following morning, our results and disposition were completely different. This time there was a tangible sense of humility. Our answers were not about letting go of possessions or things but of letting go of personal shortcomings, mistakes, failures, poor self-images, wrong doings, or excuses. Our answers were more about feelings, emotions, embarrassments and fears.

One self-image I had to let go of was that of being "Hay Seed Hank," a country boy from Utah, who was not expected to do or be anything great. While my heart was telling me to *think big*, I was covering my insecurity with the story of being this small-town character.

Step 5: Take the first step. Rather than plan out all the potential steps between where you are and where you want to be, just plan out and take the first step. Often, the closer you get to your horizon, the more perspective you have. Like with climbing a mountain, the closer you get to the next point, the more clearly you can see the best route—and usually what appears to be the top is only another horizon on the way to the top. After each step you take, ask yourself three questions: What result did I get? What did I learn? Is my horizon still the same?

My first step was to share my new horizon, goals and intentions with my wife. But the result was not what I expected. I underestimated how changing *my* goals would impact her. Since *my* goals had been *our* goals, she interpreted my expression that my *old goals* were no longer important to me as me saying that *she* was no longer as important to me. Ouch, how had I not seen and anticipated this?

We needed to work together to find a safe and satisfying route for reaching our new horizon together, one step at a time. While discovering new horizons can be exciting, you need to be flexible as you start down the paths. Indeed, the paths to get there are rarely straight.

Remember to remain focused on YOUR horizon, YOUR goal. The classic mistake is to simply accept someone else's horizon; you then find yourself wondering why you fail, are dissatisfied or have a feeling of futility. Your goals can only be achieved when they match *your* real values. Therefore, you need to have the courage to go your own way and ask your innermost self what horizons are worthwhile to aim for and spend your time and energy in pursuit of.

Thomas: *Sometimes we lose sight of our horizons.* Brendon Burchard, author of *The Charge*, writes: "When your relationships fall apart, your life falls apart." How true that is!

In situations where I lost a cherished family member through death, or when our marriage fell apart or when it became apparent that an old friend was parting ways with me—I found myself in a situation where I was unsure of my next horizon. I was trying to put my life back together, trying to find my *true north* and defining my horizon again. This never was a fun or easy process.

Many times, making connections with others and joining forces with them on the way to a new common horizon becomes a strategic moment in our life. I can still feel the magic of many of these moments today. So deep was our love, our connection and understanding, that we made plans and helped each other in shaping our future together.

Sometimes what started without boundaries, with an inspiring outlook, to reach a joint horizon, becomes increasingly difficult. From starting without barriers, a life with more and more barriers evolves.

It is a personal choice to look back and complain rather than to move on and create. It is a choice to be unhappy; a choice not to live with intent—as individuals, friends, couples, teams and organizations. Some seem to think that there is a certain reward in creating misery and complaints. Some are absolutely unaware of their subscription to unproductive thoughts and actions. If you find yourself in such a contaminated place, think again!

Still today, my heart skips a beat at all the great memories of the many strategic moments in my life. I have learned that *no matter how deep a connection, no matter how deep your wish and urge to reach a joint horizon, you will not reach it if you persist in the yesterday and in fault-finding with those you choose to partner with. Especially if you are striving to reach a common horizon as a couple.*

To go the path of a nomad towards a joint horizon requires ongoing synchronization, ongoing joyful companionship and ongoing loving support. It requires you to be strength-based, to look for the talent and contribution of your partner, your team or your friend.

So, be aware that your full wish and full heart to make it to the horizon may not be enough—it will take both of you, or all of you, if you aim for a joint horizon. As soon as one of you starts down the route of complaint and criticism, that person makes any progress towards the horizon impossible. To avoid downward-spiraling choices, make sure that you protect your heart. As you *live with intent*, you will need all your emotional energy to reach your horizon, step by step.

Who and What Do You Want to Be?

If you already know your horizon and goal, then you need to write it like this: I am becoming the store manager; I am attaining my college diploma; I am becoming an architect; I am founding a company; I am becoming a fencer.

If your horizon and goal is unclear, describe the direction in which it goes as precisely as possible. Identify yourself as the person in the goal. For example,

- I am self-employed as a consultant and advise mid-sized companies.
- I work in health care and help people who need medical assistance.
- I am a teacher and work with children.
- I am a lawyer and advise corporate clients.
- I live and work abroad.

Ask yourself whether you can reasonably reach the horizon you are reaching for. Do not waste your energy on unreachable goals. In setting your goals, you need to know your natural limitations.

Defining a goal will awaken unexpected powers within you. It will be easier to generate motivation for taking the required steps to achieve your goal. Your mental abilities may be doubled if your motivation is recharged.

Most people make the same mistake again and again: they undertake far too much for next year and far too little for the next five years. This leads to frustration and disappointment and inhibits the power that emanates from the goal—the force that enables them to access the requisite belief to reach their horizon each day.

Why do we require you to write your goals? The strength lies in the writing. When you continually write things down, six good things happen: 1) You commit yourself; 2) your goals are more defined; 3) writing goals clears your mind, creating space for other thinking processes; 4) a written goal gives you a benchmark for gauging future change and progress; 5) your personal work receives a much higher commitment; and 6) by writing your goal, you achieve a huge tactical advantage over people who try to give their best but lack a clearly-defined purpose.

Determine the Location

In navigation, knowing your current standpoint is a prerequisite for determining the path to your horizon. If you don't know where you are, how can you know how to get to where you want to go? Only when you know where you stand can you go where you want. Only when you have the courage to be honest with yourself can you find the best way to achieve your goals.

You need to take time for a "location standpoint" check! Take an inventory of your life experience, career, education, skills and knowledge—everything that makes you who you are! Include people, contacts and networks. It may turn out that you already have what you need for reaching your goal.

You also need to realize what skills you lack: perhaps patience, accuracy, language skills or perseverance. You need to gain an impression of not only what you need to start, but also what you need to finish and arrive at your end destination! When you understand what you have and also what you need, then the "mountain" that you need to climb in order to reach your determined summit will seem to get smaller.

Factors that Prevent Growth

Several factors can inhibit or prevent your growth, among them these three:

Excuse making and blame placing. As long as you are finding excuses or blaming others for why and how you ended up where you are, little in your life will change.

Expectations of perfection. It is ridiculous to say that "*everything* has to be different" or "I will change myself *completely*." That sounds determined, but is senseless and impossible. You need to make allowances for your human short-comings; otherwise, you will be disappointed with the results or with yourself and give up too fast. However, if you expect setbacks and gradual change, you can get back up when you stumble instead of giving up. Some perfectionists want so badly to have everything function perfectly that they would rather avoid trying something they think they might struggle with than failing. They fear being vulnerable, being rejected and failing. Trying to find the perfect way to do things is a problem. Putting too much energy into the strategic planning of a goal is like *dry swimming* or trying to learn how to ski by reading books—it will not help us to reach our destination and not teach us things. Since **good is the enemy of best,** you should first aim for the good and let it gradually, step by step, take over and encompass your life.

Ingratitude. The key to change is to be grateful and express gratitude for all that has brought you to where you are today and for everyone and everything that has made you who you are up to this point.

Lack of discipline. Once you recognize the need to change and are motivated to change, you next need to exercise a daily language discipline. If you use the words *forever, never* and *always*, you will inevitably experience difficulties and fail in the long run.

Remember, horizons are constantly on the move. The closer you come to your horizon, the more clearly you can see the next one. Keep moving and choosing new horizons that matter.

> *"The purest form of insanity is to leave everything as it is*
> *and at the same time hope that something changes."*
> *~ Albert Einstein*

TIP

SEE—Your Next Horizon

What topics will accompany you through your life? Where will the journey take you?

Answer these questions: What fascinates me? What do I enjoy doing? What can I do well? What would I like to learn? What would I enjoy being able to do? What have I always wanted to do? How have I always imagined my life to be? Where and with whom do I feel the most comfortable? What outside of my career is important to me?

Don't be a gambler—be an investor!

Discover your long-term goals. What do you want to accomplish in five to ten years? What are your three to five most important long-term goals?

Main Objective 1 (long-term)

On a scale of 0 to 100 percent, where are you in relation to achieving this goal today? Where do you want to be in a year or more?

Status today	Year 1	Year 2	Year 3	Year 4	Year 5	Year 6	Year 7

What actions and what steps will lead to you accomplishing this goal?

Main Objective 2 (long-term)

On a scale of 0 to 100 percent, where are you in relation to achieving this goal today? Where do you want to be in a year or more?

Status today	Year 1	Year 2	Year 3	Year 4	Year 5	Year 6	Year 7

What actions and what steps will lead to you accomplishing this goal?

Main Objective 3 (long-term)

On a scale of 0 to 100 percent, where are you in relation to achieving this goal today? Where do you want to be in a year or more?

Status today	Year 1	Year 2	Year 3	Year 4	Year 5	Year 6	Year 7

What actions and what steps will lead to you accomplishing this goal?

Main Objective 4 (long-term)
On a scale of 0 to 100 percent, where are you in relation to this goal today? Where do you want to be in a year or more?

Status today	Year 1	Year 2	Year 3	Year 4	Year 5	Year 6	Year 7

What actions and what steps will lead to you accomplishing this goal?

Main Objective 5 (long-term)
On a scale of 0 to 100 percent, where are you in relation to achieving this goal today? Where do you want to be in a year or more?

Status today	Year 1	Year 2	Year 3	Year 4	Year 5	Year 6	Year 7

What actions and what steps will lead to you accomplishing this goal?

Set your goals for the *year*. What do you want to accomplish this year? What are the five most important goals this year?

126

Goal for this year—Number 1

On a scale of 0 to 100 percent, where are you in relation to this goal today? Where do you want to be in a year?

Date	Status Today	In One Year
	%	%

What actions and what steps will lead to you accomplishing this goal?

Goal for this year—Number 2

On a scale of 0 to 100 percent, where are you in relation to this goal today? Where do you want to be in a year?

Date	Status Today	In One Year
	%	%

What actions and what steps will lead to this goal being completed?

Goal for this year—Number 3

On a scale of 0 to 100 percent, where are you in relation to this goal today? Where do you want to be in a year?

Date	Status Today	In One Year
	%	%

What actions and what steps will lead to you accomplishing this goal?

Goal for this year—Number 4

On a scale of 0 to 100 percent, where are you in relation to achieving this goal today? Where do you want to be in a year?

Date	Status Today	In One Year
	%	%

What actions and what steps will lead to this goal?

Goal for this year—Number 5

On a scale of 0 to 100 percent, where are you in relation to accomplishing this goal today? Where do you want to be in a year?

Date	Status Today	In One Year
	%	%

DO—To immediately improve your career and quality of life, concentrate on four areas:

1. Do *more* of the things that make you happier and that you consider valuable.
2. Do *less* of the things that you see as hindrances or obstacles to you in achieving your goals.
3. Do *new* things that you have never done before and set a new course in your life.
4. Stop doing certain things that do not fit into your life.

What actions and what steps will lead to these objectives and goals? Complete the following exercises and then be ready to attack your goals!

Important: Since "even the best strategy degenerates from a certain point to simply becoming work," be prepared to roll up your sleeves and get going!

Additional exercises

Make a goal collage. Create a visual image of your goals. A goal collage is an image that shows your desires and goals for the coming year. You will need: scissors; a glue stick; a large piece of paper; and many different magazines and newspapers. Think about your goal for the next year and picture it in your mind's eye. Take a magazine of your choice and go through it. Whenever you see an image, word or phrase that you like, cut it out. Repeat this process using several different magazines and newspapers. Eventually, you will have a wealth of pictures and words. Then start to stick the pictures to the paper so that a finished image emerges. Make sure that everything important to you is included in the picture (business success, family, health, etc.).

Examples of goal collages.

Creative writing exercise. Set a timer for seven minutes. Put on music that inspires you and ask yourself the question: *"If time and money did not matter, what would I do with my life now and also in the future?"* As you think about this question, start writing whatever comes into your mind. Do not interrupt the flow of writing until the time is up. You will likely discover some unexpected good and useful ideas for your goals. Wait a few days and then repeat the exercise using a different piece of music.

GROW—The following *affirmations* and *checklist* will accelerate your growth.

Affirmations
- You have the freedom to create your plan yourself.
- You have the strength to devote yourself to your dreams and desires.
- Your life plan acts as a reliable compass and directs your path.
- Your plan for this year is the autopilot of your success.
- You have a healthy balance between plans and spontaneity.
- You have a clear vision of where you are going but are flexible in response to new opportunities.

Do not be discouraged: even if your goal exceeds your current capabilities, your sincere efforts will bring the goal closer. Think of your goal daily and imagine the benefits that you will receive from its accomplishment. Look forward to your first successes and visualize what your fulfilled goal looks and feels like.

> *"Until one is committed, there is hesitancy, the chance to draw back. Concerning all acts of initiative (and creation), there is one elementary truth, the ignorance of which kills countless ideas and splendid plans: that the moment one definitely commits oneself, then providence moves too. All sorts of things occur to help one that would never otherwise have occurred. A whole stream of events issues from the*

*decision, raising in one's favor all manner of unforeseen
incidents and meetings and material assistance, which no
man could have dreamed would have come his way. I have
learned a deep respect for one of Goethe's couplets: Whatever
you can do, or dream you can do, begin it. Boldness has
genius, power, and magic in it. Begin it now."*
~ *William Hutchison Murray*

Checklist
1. I will establish a learning diary.
2. I will establish my personal five-year plan.
3. I will determine my goals for this year.
4. I will set SMART goals: Specific, Measurable, Achievable, Realistic, Time-based.
5. I will establish my goal-achievement timeline for the stages of my goal planning.
6. I will compare my goals with my values and personal attitude.
7. I will visualize my horizon and goals with collages.
8. I will stay open-minded and ready to take advantage of fresh opportunities.

CHAPTER 6
VISUALIZATION

SHAPE YOUR FUTURE

EVERY MOMENT OF YOUR LIFE IS INFINITELY CREATIVE AND THE UNIVERSE IS **ENDLESSLY BOUNTIFUL.** JUST PUT FORTH A CLEAR ENOUGH REQUEST, AND EVERYTHING **YOUR HEART TRULY DESIRES** MUST COME **TO YOU.**

SHAKTI GAWAIN

Now that your goals are concrete, you can use **VISUALIZATION to bring your goals to life.** Principle 6, **Visualization**, is symbolized by the liquid state. **Going with the flow** as you visualize the realization of your goal will bring **FLEXIBILITY** to the implementation of your goal.

Visualization means using your **IMAGINATION** to see your success and how to arrive there.

As you visualize reaching your goals, pay attention to how you feel and the language you use. In Principle 7, **Language Creates Reality,** we will go **DEEPER** into the topic of how to use language in achieving your goals.

The best way to shape your future is to **visualize it—and then CREATE IT**.

Thomas: I was 14 when I learned to fly a glider and was very impressed with the systemic procedures of the take-off, flight and landing requirements. Among many of the notable instructors, one military pilot named Wagner made a great impression on me. He told us that when we went to bed each evening we should sit in our beds and mentally go through a complete take-off, flight and landing. This way we would learn the necessary skills much faster and better.

By learning this technique, even when there was bad weather and we were unable to fly for one or two weekends, our training program was not substantially disrupted. We made "dry runs" in our minds and visually made hundreds of successful take offs and landings.

Today I regularly speak professionally in front of different people—in both small groups and large audiences. I have never held an event either as a coach or lecturer without having intensely visualized the scene in advance. Whenever possible, I go into the room I will be speaking in the night before so as to get a feel for the space and to make the visualization even stronger. By the time I'm actually speaking the next day, the work and procedures are already familiar to me, just as the take-offs and landings were when I was 14!

No matter whom you are, no matter what you do, your success depends largely on your imagination. You can use visualization to harness your mental capacity to realize what you want in your life. You likely already use this method but have not yet developed an awareness of it (see the chapter on *autosuggestion*). This method is neither new nor unusual nor strange. In fact, you use this force constantly, even if you are unaware of it.

How can you systematically build and strengthen the power of your imagination now? The more hobbies or interests you have, the more enhanced are your problem-solving abilities. The more you practice doing things, the more you can find workable solutions. Your brain becomes enriched with various possibilities and makes stronger cross-linked connections.

Likewise, traveling educates you. The more cultures you experience, the wider your background, the more operative and reasoning alternative solutions you will find. Your various interests enrich your inner reserves from which your imagination springs. Varied interests in the real world spark your imagination—the ability to mentally create an idea or an image in your mind. When you visualize, you use your imagination to give rise to the mental picture of what is to come or what you wish for the future.

Justin: In spring 1985, at the age of 17, I had a vision. I was in Sundance, Utah, sitting in a lounge chair outside a beautiful house, enjoying the sunshine and the specter of skiers gliding down the slopes. I remember the stunning view filled with snow-capped mountain peaks under a deep blue sky. I thought of my future horizon and spoke the wish out loud: "I want to live in Sundance, Utah." Eight years later, two weeks before my wedding, I received a call about a property management opportunity available at the Sundance Institute in Utah. I followed the lead, and as I approached the home that I was to manage, I recognized the deck with the yellow chairs immediately. It was the very house that I had visited that spring day in 1985. I took the job and my wife and I lived there for the next six years.

Your life is moving towards what you constantly say to yourself. Be *for* yourself, not against yourself. Change your words, change your world. See that your life matters by choosing your horizons intentionally and your words carefully, so that you can *Live with Intent.*

The objectives for visualization can be found on all levels of your life: in your personal life and career, and in all other situations and relationships.

Take Five Steps

The following five steps will help you to achieve remarkable success with visualization:

1. Concentrate on one idea at a time; channel that idea into a positive image. Continue to put power and energy into the visualization of this image until your wish comes true.

2. Set a target for your visualization; identify a measurable objective of what you want to achieve. With the help of visualization, identify what you want to achieve; whether it is an object, event, situation or circumstance in your life that you want to change. In the beginning, choose something that poses as little resistance as possible. As you become more experienced with visualization, you will become more confident and able to tackle more complicated things.

3. Get an accurate picture of what you want to achieve in your mind. Imagine how it will be, both physically and mentally. As with autosuggestion, go confidently and naturally into visualization and assume that the desire is already a reality. Make sure that you consider all the details within your mind's eye.

4. Repeatedly focus on this mental image. During the day and in relaxed settings, reflect regularly on your mental picture. Do not force yourself to think of the picture or use excessive energy; instead let the desired outcome just flow over you.

5. Give your goal positive power and energy. You need to have a positive attitude about visualization and give yourself only positive messages (affirmations). Never question the exercise or do it half-heartedly. Like a small plant, your project requires constant loving care and protection. If doubts or concerns arise, let them blow away as if swept up by the wind. Cultivate and maintain this mental image. Tell yourself over and over again that it is possible to achieve what you are visualizing.

Visualization is essential for top athletes. **Steven Nyman**, a friend and Olympian with three World Cup Champion titles, uses visualization when he's preparing for a downhill skiing competition. At the starting gate, we often see racers leaning forward over their poles with their eyes shut. With their feet planted firmly on the ground, their heads and bodies are slowly swaying back and forth. Meanwhile, in their minds, they are moving at race speeds exceeding 150 kilometers per hour, faster than the terminal velocity of a free-falling skydiver! These daring speed racers visualize every turn, corner and jump on the course. Amazingly, they finish their imaginary run within seconds of their actual time. World Cup Downhill races of over two minutes are often won by 1/100th of a second. Every movement of the body affects whether you win or lose the race. While downhill racers have only two practice runs down the course before the race, they may have visualized the race in every detail hundreds of times.

Steven started dreaming of skiing in the Olympics as a young boy. Then he visualized his way to back-to-back National Downhill championships in 2004 and 2005. From there, he visualized his way through serious injuries and three World Cup Championships in 2006, 2012 and 2014. He is now visualizing his fourth time as an Olympian in the 2018 winter Olympics!

Once your goal has been reached, make yourself fully aware of the end achievement. Give thanks and then proceed, when necessary or possible, with gratitude, to the next goal. If you are a ski racer, be glad to have finished the course unharmed!

In business, visualizations have been a best practice for many years. They are used daily, from the preparation of presentations to the visualization of details for decision-making.

"Simplicity is the highest perfection," declared Leonardo da Vinci during the Renaissance. Steve Jobs, one of the greatest visionaries in recent memory, helped to revive and successfully apply this attitude in the digital age around Simplicity as the ultimate sophistication.

TIP

SEE—According to Gawain[30], the success of your creative visualizing depends on three factors:

your desire

your faith,

and your acceptance.

---

30 Gawain, S., *Creative Visualization*, Whatever Publishing, Mill Valley, California, USA, 1978

Intention

The desire to achieve the objective must come from within you. It must come not out of greed or the desire to acquire more possessions, but out of a clear goal-orientated feeling.

The intersection of all three factors can be referred to as your intention. Your intention is the fixed, absolute determination to implement something, to realize something. The more the intention is supported by desire, faith and acceptance—the faster and easier the visualization will take root and create results in your life.

DO—**Ask yourself the fundamental questions:** 1) *From the bottom of my heart, do I really want to achieve this goal?* The basis of accomplishing this goal is the inner necessity to want to achieve it and to be able to achieve it; 2) *Do I really believe in this goal? Do I believe that I can accomplish it?* Cultivating the faith to be able to achieve this goal can be compared to caring for a young plant. It needs caretaking, water and nutrients. Doubt and concerns rob it of the necessary nutrients needed for healthy growth. Harboring doubts about the goal means sabotaging our own success. We need to fully expect to reach our goals. Doubts are likely to come at some point along the way. Sometimes your long-range goals can seem to disappear. If they do, go step by step. Bring into focus your next step and make it happen. Use each step to build momentum for the next step.

Justin: The best example I know of someone going step by step is my wife Jenny. When she approached 40 years old, she began to doubt nearly everything in her life: Her role as a wife, mother, business owner. Her horizon, her goals, and her sense of purpose seemed to evaporate, leaving her depressed, anxious and deeply unhappy. The only thing she could see was her next step, which was to move from Switzerland back to the USA. After more than a decade living abroad, she needed a break.

Once back in the USA, she became clear about her next step: getting control of her eating and losing 60 pounds. She felt limited by her body and knew this would limit her happiness.

So she started Crossfit, an intense fitness regimen supported by a strong community. She lost the weight, and like magic her next step appeared. She became certified as a Crossfit coach and began coaching several days a week. While doing so, she discovered a unique talent in coaching people in Olympic style weightlifting; the Clean and Jerk, and the Snatch. She loved the technical aspect of movement needed to complete these lifts. Several coaching certifications later, she started her own Olympic Weightlifting gym. She is now 46 years old, has her own Weightlifting team that competes nationally. In 2017, she was elected onto the Board of Directors of USA Weightlifting, the highest governing body of Olympic Weightlifting in the USA.

Step by step, your horizon and goals will become a reality.

    A. Visualize your dream home: Design your dream home—first in your head, then on paper—as you would build it, if money and time were not a limiting factor. This is a creative exercise. Maybe you will have fun and enjoy doing it and it will open up a new creative side in you.

    B. Visualize a difficult conversation. In preparing for a difficult conversation, negotiation, interview, trial, or other challenging encounter—imagine that you execute the call confidently, calmly and with competence. Create the picture of an excellent result in your mind's eye.

    C. Visualize your desires. First, look at something that you desire. Choose something simple that seems easily attainable. This can be an object, event, situation or circumstance in your life that you would like to change. Take some time and relax, making sure that you are comfortable. Now concentrate on relaxing your whole body, limb by limb. Be mentally aware of the different parts of your body. Begin with your hands: relax your fingertips, your fingers, your hands, forearms, elbows, upper arms; next relax your shoulders, chest, neck, head, face and ears; finally, relax your abdomen, pelvis, buttocks, thighs, knees, lower legs, feet and toes. Breathe deeply and slowly throughout this whole exercise.

In this state of relaxation, visualize your desire. Paint the mental picture as accurately as possible; consider its shape, its color. If it is an object, imagine how you operate or use it. Use the same technique to imagine the desired event or situation. Describe how it will be for you, how you will feel, what you will say, what you will tell your family and friends, etc.

Continue with this exercise for as long as you enjoy doing it. This time frame can be anything between five minutes and an hour.

D. Treasure Maps. Creating and working with treasure maps is very effective. The goal collage is similar to the treasure map in that it is as real as possible, and it is a specifically-crafted image of a desired state. Again, you have a tool that enables you to put positive energy and strength toward your goal achievement. The treasure map is like a blueprint of a product. It can be drawn, painted or created like a collage, or it can be something as simple as a picture from a magazine or a book. The treasure map shows what it might be like to see the goal fully realized. As with the goal collage, your intent in creating treasure maps is not to create a work of art, but rather to capture the relevant content.

The following points will help you in creating effective treasure maps:

- Each treasure map should only represent one goal or aspect of your life.
- The map size is arbitrary. You might create your maps in the same format as *Live with Intent* so you can always have them with you as you study the chapters. You may like to take them to a copy shop, get the pages laminated and bind them in a folder with metal rings to facilitate turning the pages.
- Use lots of color and expression.
- Do not use negative or unwanted objects; show the exclusive, ideal and desired state.
- Write an image sub-title that positively summarizes the whole picture. For example: "Here I am on a cruise on the ship MS Europa with my family. I really like it, and

I have enough money to enjoy many different cities and countries."

- If you work digital, there are many apps for visualizing your treasure maps. Customized treasure maps bring your visualized goal much closer!

Remember to find a few minutes regularly to "get in touch" with your treasure maps. Review them in peace and solitude. Regularly think about them. The rest is done without your effort!

Affirmations

- You can vividly imagine how good your life is and will continue to be.
- You are taking your life and transforming it into a piece of art.
- Everything you need is already within you.
- Achieving your goals is easy and effortless to you.
- It's okay for you to have everything you aspire to have.

Apply these affirmations multiple times a day for a minimum of two weeks.

Checklist

1. Use these five steps to achieve remarkable success in visualization: 1) Concentrate on one idea, applied to a positive image; 2) set a specific goal—a measurable parameter you want to achieve; 3) create a certain image of the goal in your mind; 4) regularly focus on this mental image; and 5) strengthen goals with positive power and energy for a positive attitude and feedback.
2. Visualize your dream house, apartment, office, or surroundings.
3. Visualize two difficult conversations in advance. Depending on the challenge, imagine how you hold the conversation with confidence and competence. In preparation for a difficult conversation, a negotiation, an interview or trial, create the image of an excellent result in your mind.

4. Implement digital and analogous tools for lifting your thoughts, notes and visualizations to a new level. Analogous tools include: notebooks; moleskins; sketch books; diaries with visualizations; treasure maps and collages. Digital tools include, amongst many others: software for notes (Evernote); software for mind maps (Mindmanager); software for visual task management (Droptask, taskworld, Trello); and software for collaboration and team management (Trello, taskworld, Wrike, ToDo-Ist, Asana).

CHAPTER 7

LANGUAGE CREATES REALITY

INSPIRE PEOPLE

> THE STROKE OF THE WHIP MAKES A **MARK** IN THE FLESH, BUT THE **STROKE OF A TONGUE** BREAKS **BONES**.

APOCRYPHA

Since "language creates reality,"[31] we all need to pay **close attention to our SPEECH**. What you say and how you say it, has an **enormous potential creative POWER**. Our reality is strongly influenced by our language.

Continually repeated phrases become **REALITY**. Through **repetition** they become a matter of course and will; at some point, they become **externally manifest**.

A "bad word" may spoil you and your family's whole day, maybe even a whole weekend or week. We've all experienced the ill-effects of vulgar, obscene, condescending, abusive and offensive language. So many conflicts and **EMOTIONAL** injuries could be avoided through **conscious language** usage and **healthy and meaningful dialogue**.

[31]Paul Watzlawick is an author and representative of the so-called radical (uncompromising) constructivism—a position within the so-called theory of knowledge. He teaches that a perception is not a reflection of a mind-independent reality, but "reality" is, according to the constructivists, always a construction of sensory stimuli and memory for each individual. Therefore, objectivity in the sense of a match of the perceived (constructed) image and reality is impossible—every perception is completely subjective.

Thomas: When I was 11 years old and in the fifth grade, everything was still new to me. On a daily basis, I felt excited and filled with optimism and pride about being the new kid in the "Gymnasium"[32] (secondary school). It was a big, new world, and I was right in the middle of it. The first days and weeks of school were exciting, and the teachers remarkably well qualified. Three decades later, I still remember the experience very clearly.

I was part of a special project, one that was observed by both the media and the school ministry. Our lessons in German, Art and Music were combined to make one single subject. So we heard, for example, the orchestral composition Moldova of the Czech composer Bedřich Smetana. We dealt with the score, then wrote an essay on the topic and painted a picture of the symphonic poem. Since our teacher, Mr. Gutfleisch, was also part of the school management, we had great respect for his authority. We respectfully listened with reverential silence whenever he told us about what the secondary school was like and what we would need to do to pass our final exams one distant day.

One day, after convincing each of us that we could sing, he called us individually to the front of the class, handed us a sheet of music and asked each of us to sing. I barely got a sound out of my throat. I hoped that Mr. Gutfleisch would show me what I should do, because I showed no talent for singing. As I stood in front of the class, the light shining directly on me, Mr. Gutfleisch shook his head hopelessly and said: "Dear class, the fact that we all can learn to sing does not mean that everybody in this class can sing. Thank you, Thomas, you may sit down!" His comment has stayed with me for 35 years!

---

32 Gymnasium is part of the three-tiered secondary school system in Germany. Hauptschule is for those more practically minded, Realschule is for those not wanting to concentrate fully on Academia and Gymnasium is for the Academics. The Abitur is the equivalent to the College Diploma and the English A Levels and is necessary to achieve before going on to University.

Within seconds my world fell apart. It was not so much *what* he said but *how* he said it. He seemed convinced that I was incapable of singing. He said it with such a strong energy and conviction. I was devastated. Why wasn't I allowed to learn how to sing? I really enjoyed school and learning, so why should I be excluded from learning this subject? His criticism hurt and for the next 35 years I was not able to sing a note in tune. Moreover, his message was not given out of love, wisdom, concern or desire to help—or at least I didn't receive his message in that spirit—even though he was in many ways also an outstanding and remarkable teacher.

Such criticisms leave behind deep scars. Recipients pay the price, perhaps for the rest of their lives.

> *"Without any selfish ulterior motives, you can point out others' mistakes with affection and well meaning, but even if one tells the truth it can still pierce the heart. Therefore, my advice which comes from the heart is, 'choose gentle words.'"*
> *~ Longchen Rabjam*

"A gentle answer turns away wrath."

Proverbs 15:1(NASB)

In business, saying the wrong word at the wrong time might not only destroy a career, it might also destroy lives and jobs and drive companies into bankruptcy, as the following example shows.

Dr. Rolf-Ernst Breuer, *former CEO of Deutsche Bank, experienced this principle painfully and personally. A momentous television interview was followed by years of litigation with the Kirch family and resulted in a 2015 settlement of over 925 million euros in damages.*[33] *This interview, which was broadcast on Bloomberg TV on February 4, 2002, is translated below in its original wording:*

Interviewer: *Kirch is in a lot of debt, in very high debt. How exposed is the Deutsche Bank?"*

Dr. Rolf-Ernst Breuer: *Relatively comfortable I would say, because—which is known and since I am committing no indiscretion if I tell that—the credit that we have is numerically not among the largest, but relatively in the middle area and fully secured by a lien on Kirch's shares in the Springer Publishing House. Thus, nothing can actually happen to us; we feel well secured. It's never nice, if a debtor is in trouble, and I hope that's not the case. But if that would be so, we would not have to worry.*

Interviewer: *The question is whether one could do more to keep him going.*

Dr. Rolf-Ernst Breuer: *I think this is relatively questionable. If all you read about and hear about is true, the financial sector is not ready to take on further debt or even make our own resources available if the situation remains the same. Therefore, if debt relief is necessary, it*

---

33 See Spiegel Online, *Prozess in München: Ex-Deutsche-Bank-Chef Breuer verteidigt Kirch-Interview*, 07/28/2015, http://www.spiegel.de/wirtschaft/unternehmen/ex-deutsche-bank-chef-breuer-verteidigt-kirch-interview-a-1045644.html, accessed on 08/25/2015

can only come from a third party, who is interested in supporting him as you say."[34]

"*I did neither want to send out signals nor cause harm,*" Breuer said in his defense in July 2015. "*I had only spoken the truth.*" He went on to say: "*I never wanted to hurt the Kirch Group and had not been aware of the consequences. Harming one of the bank's customers through an interview would have never crossed my mind.*"[35]

However, the presiding judge, Peter Noll, had his doubts: "Aren't you aware of the fact that speaking the truth—expressed at the wrong place and time—can be a mistake?"

Thomas: The wrong word at the wrong time not only led to a corporate bankruptcy, it also resulted in a financial loss amounting to almost one billion euros for Deutsche Bank. That should be a warning to us. I met Mr. Breuer during his time as CEO; we had lunch together in Frankfurt. I was impressed by his professionalism and strategic clarity on the future of the banking sector. Had a dilettante, by his language, evoked an unwanted reality? No, here a professional manager with multi-supervisory board capabilities and a remarkable background in law and banking had unfortunately tainted his legacy. And he'd done it with three sentences only, as listed in the previous page! To me, this story is even sadder because I appreciate him as a person.

The tongue is a small part of the body, and yet it boasts of great things. The wrong word is like a fire. See how great a forest is set aflame by such a small fire! Like a rudder, the tongue sets the course of our life.[36] If we are to direct our lives

---

34 See www.abendblatt.de, *Wortlaut des Interviews mit Rolf Breuer zu Kirch,* http://www.abendblatt.de/wirtschaft/article107750348/Wortlaut-des-Interviews-with-Rolf-Breuer-zu-Kirch.html, accessed on 08/26/2015

35 Cf. bos/dpa/Reuters in Spiegel Online, Prozess in München: *Ex-DeutscheBank-ChefBreuer verteidigt Kirch-Interview,* 07/28/2015, http://www.spiegel.de/wirtschaft/unternehmen/ex-deutsche-bank-chef-breuer-verteidigt-kirch-interview-a-1045644.html, accessed on 08/25/2015

36 See Spiegel Online, Prozess in München: Ex-Deutsche-Bank-Chef Breuer verteidigt Kirch-Interview, 07/28/2015, http://www.spiegel.de/wirtschaft/unternehmen/ex-deutsche-bank-chef-breuer-verteidigt-kirch-interview-a-1045644.html, accessed on 08/25/2015

and the lives around us toward greatness, we must bridle our tongues, just as we need to bridle a horse.

The power of our words will determine the outcomes of our lives.
Alexander F. Macdonald, born in Scotland 1825, was the first Mayor of Mesa, Arizona; he was also the great-great-great grandfather of Justin[37]:

A terrific rainstorm struck suddenly and fiercely. For a half hour it poured while the lightning flashed and the thunder crashed, at the end of which time the whole country was under water, and a river that would "swim a calf" ran between our house and the corral. No sooner than the rain clouds had lifted than we saw A.F. Macdonald coming from town. He was alone in an open buckboard, and I've never seen anyone or anything look so drenched as he did. His hat brim dripped over his ears, his beard was sodden and his clothes were streaming with water. Still he was feebly urging his mules to make haste and get him to shelter. "He'll never make it through that torrent," my mother said as we gazed at him, and we both shouted out to him to wait until the flood had subsided. But he was too chilled to heed us and continued to urge his mules toward us.

He probably would have driven them right through if they'd done his bidding. But they didn't. They got to the edge of the stream and then stopped, flinching when he rapped them smartly with his whip, shaking their heads and all but rearing when he prodded them further. Fearful that they'd overturn the buckboard in their stubborn resistance, I took off my shoes and stockings, seized an oak stick to help me keep my balance, and waded through the stream to him. The water was almost waist deep and ran swift and angry. But I made it through to him and got hold of the mule's bridle bits. They quieted down a little as soon as I had a firm hold on them and began to talk quietly to them. A few minutes later they were under control

---

37   Macdonald was acknowledged for the power of his words in a family memoir by Nelle Spilsbury Hatch, a young girl in the community.

so I led them through the stream. It was a flash flood and was falling fast. Even in the short time I was with them it had noticeably lowered, and getting them to follow me through the water was relatively easy. I led them into the door yard where mother helped him from his seat and had him by a cozy fire in a jiffy. I took care of his mules and then carried his wet bedding and lunch box in the house.

He never let me forget that incident. "I've never seen so welcome a sight in all my days," he'd say again and again, "as the sight of that girl making her way to me through that flood. I've never been more in need of just that kind of help. You reminded me of my daughter Bessie, always on hand to help in any way needed." That was the pay for me. To be likened to one whose praises I had heard sung so much was music to my ears. It was a stimulus that bore me up and really put me in the clouds. He kept me there too.

Nothing I did after that was noted by him, and the first thing I knew I was half believing that maybe I did have character— maybe with it I could find an opening into a better life than just ranching. Maybe if I kept hoping, something would turn up for me better than milking cows, hoeing corn, feeding pigs. Maybe I could go back to school, maybe graduate and then— but farther than that I couldn't see. But his casual remarks had awakened something that changed my whole outlook on life, and gave me an incentive that never died.

Funny isn't it, what little things can change the current of a stream. Or what a few words of praise can do to one so starved for them. I also wondered: Did he realize the magnitude of the effect those few words had on my life?

If you want to know what you'll be like five years from now, simply listen to what you're saying about yourself today. What if we thought about ourselves the same way our biggest fans thought about us? What if we talked to ourselves the same way we talked about our heroes, our loved ones and our dearest friends? What if we recognized our accomplishments regardless of their size?

When negative thoughts come to mind, don't make the mistake of verbalizing them. The moment you speak them, they begin to take root. Success and failure are in the power of our words. You believe what you say about yourself more than you believe what others say about you. Your thoughts lead to words that determine where you go, who goes with you, and what value you create. Use your words to change situations rather than to describe them. The more you talk about something, the more you draw it in. Therefore, talk about solutions, not problems. Talk about victory, not defeat. Talk about strengths, not weaknesses. Talk about the way you want to be, not the way you are. Change from the inside out. Once you get a picture of your horizon on the inside, it can come to pass on the outside. This does not mean that we need to hide negative or discouraging thoughts that will bubble up. Treat them like clouds that will pass on. Just do not fixate on them continually by speaking about them.

Language—the nature of your speech and your choice of words—also has the power to influence the Law of Attraction. For example, surely you have at some point met an extraordinary person—someone who you notice straightaway is special. Notice how much their skillful use of language and dialogue affect their first impression.

Ask yourself: What messages did you send out yesterday or today to your loved ones, your children, partners, or colleagues? Were they messages of encouragement? Did they lift and inspire those around you? Did they help lead you toward your horizon? When we say the wrong things, what do we bring into the minds of others and what do we bring into our environment?

If you were aware of the impression you make on others and your environment, you would speak every sentence as you really mean it. You would not say to a colleague: "Today you need to shake a leg," but, "I think you could do your work a little better today." And rather than use the ubiquitous term "Oh great," which sarcastically reinforces praise even when something has gone wrong, you might admit, "Oh, no, I didn't do it right."

Some modern teaching is focused on our right to "wish" and wishing thoughts that create our worlds; this philosophy suggests that we can thus make orders to the universe and that what we want will manifest itself. That, however, is typically not enough. In our experience, we must both see what we wish for and do our part in making it a reality.

We value the viewpoint expressed in the *New Testament*, in John 1:1-3, "In the beginning was the Word, and the Word was with God, and the Word was God. The same was in the beginning with God. All things were made by him; and without him was not anything made that was made." And in the *Old Testament* of the Bible (Genesis 1:3) we read: "God said, 'Let there be light,' and there was light."

Since we are not God and lack the power and authority of divinity, our words won't have the same impact; however, when we vocalize a desire, we send an arrow in the direction of our goal. The power of the archer determines how fast the arrow flies.

Yes, the spoken word creates your reality and certainly has more creative power than we are aware. We see this again and again in autosuggestion and in daily dialogue at work, at home with the family, and in our society. The first sensory organ that develops in the human body after the fusion of the sperm and egg is the ear! Just a few days after fertilization, the ears are formed; and in the sixth week of pregnancy the outer, middle and inner ear are developed.[38] Even though our primary ability is the ability to hear, the sense of sight tends to be more valued in our culture.

Studies show that people who lose their sight generally find a way to work around the loss of sight. In contrast, people who lose their hearing tend to lose various other skills, like self-perception, and thus they are more easily jostled around. To gain a sense of the importance of hearing, try this experiment: buy some earplugs and seal your ears. Now go about your daily activities—such as doing housework, clearing out the

---

38   Braun, Susann Theresa, *Achte auf das, was Du sagst*, vianova, 2012

dishwasher or cooking something. See how difficult it is to be aware of things around you and of how much you unconsciously do rely on sounds to give you orientation and feedback. See how it impacts your perception of your surroundings.

Tomatis[39] writes: "The basis of all experience is the tone of life that is communicated to the embryo through the body, especially from the mother's voice, and to which it responds. The success of the dialogue (before birth) is the first requirement for affirmation of life and ability to love." At birth, the baby is already familiar with words and language. The brain and the ability to think develop much more after birth.

Language and vocabulary have an earlier influence on the development of people than thoughts. This fact underscores how important language is. The tone of the parents' voices is decisive in the development of the child. Expressing a loving and genuine vocabulary releases fear and tension within the recipient. This applies to communication with people of all ages in both private and professional environments.

Have you ever noticed how elderly women talk to babies? They speak in a way that is distinct, clear, positive, full of expectation; and while the babies listen, their larynxes resonate in a way, as if they themselves would have formed the words!

Language has a big impact in relationships. The language in partnership and in marriage reveals its status. You can choose to use a language with your partner that is cold and unemotional or one that is tender and loving. Whichever language you select and use will have an impact on the mood of your partner. Your words have tremendous power. They can help to create a happy mood, give energy, and make someone feel capable of doing extraordinary things. Or they can have the opposite effect and make someone feel paralyzed.

The words we say really matter! Whenever we speak, whether good or bad, we are giving life to what we are saying. Use your words intentionally to attach vision to your horizon. Your words have creative power. The stories we tell ourselves and others become part of our horizon.

---

39 Tomatis, Alfred A., Der Klang des Lebens, rororo Taschenbuch, 2000

Food for Thought

The goal of communication is to have a common dialogue, to impart messages, to have free exchanges, to form opinions, to understand, to be understood, to seek truth and to reflect. Good communication creates an exchange that brings people together and creates connections. In successful communication, we find recognition, affirmation, attention, security to express our thoughts and feelings, and mutual understanding.

Use the right words at the right time. One-way communication can bring a great deal of irritation and hurt feelings. Unfortunately, when communicating, many people adopt an attitude of seeking first to be understood, which often leads to problems. They are obsessed with expressing their concerns, their thoughts, their need to bring their own ideas to the table—essentially wanting to be understood. However, this attitude in a speaker usually leads to an attitude of indifference in an audience—people stop listening.

Sometimes we see a struggle for one point of view to prevail over another. In the end, no one is listening; hence, no dialogue takes place. Instead of being enriched and edified, both parties just "push their own views." In worst cases, power struggles, misunderstandings and irritations ensue. This tragic consequence, of course, is also an opportunity for change and development.

Seek first to understand. When you seek first to understand, you communicate with a different attitude. Your personal magnetism, attractiveness and charisma—as well as your ability to be in a relationship with other people—will improve enormously. As you apply this principle of *empathy*, you change your perspective—your goal within the dialogue. You do not try first to be understood by the other person; instead, you try first to understand, then to be understood. You go into a conversation with the attitude of wanting first and most to understand your counterpart.

Note that *empathy* is not the same as *sympathy*! **Sympathy** implies affection (or affectation), while **empathy** is the sincere attempt to recognize and understand another person's thoughts, emotions, intentions and personality traits. The aim of empathy is to genuinely understand the other person and convey to them that they are understood. One way you can achieve this aim is by restating the initial content, perhaps using other words. This is also referred to as "active listening."

For example, to ensure you understand correctly what your conversation partner said, you might say: "If I understand correctly, that means...," or "Have I understood that you mean that...," or "Did you want to say that..." You speak in full sincerity and gentleness.

You can also explain feelings that you perceive as follows:
- "I have the impression that it is about... Is this correct?"
- "I have the feeling that I have not fully understood precisely what it is about..."
- "If I have understood you correctly, then this means that..."
- "Have I understood that you..."
- "How do you feel at the moment?"
- "I am aware that you..."
- "You probably felt..."
- "You are giving the impression of saying..."

When there is much at stake and the subject is emotionally charged, you need to communicate with empathy and conduct the conversation with restraint. Communication can easily be questioned, mislead or misconstrued. You can counteract this tendency by mentally repeating what you've heard and only ask questions if you have the feeling that you have not completely understood it. Be honest with yourself and with others. Ask yourself daily how you can improve your communication. The ensuing conversations will lead to good relationships and results.

Your goal is to cultivate a genuine and open exchange of views—not to resort to extreme loud and verbal violence or to silence and retreat.

Effective dialogue modulates in the middle. On one side we have the emotional escalation of volume; on the other side the quiet treatment. You improve the dialogue—the flow of understanding between two people—by listening ("two ears, one mouth") to their concerns.

Ben Zander, one of the top music coaches and conductors, is famous for his uncanny ability to coach students, whom he has met for the first time, before live audiences. At the Pop Tech conference in 2008, he taught the audience[40] a profound truth about two different worlds and dialogues in which people live. The first world he called *the downward spiral*, which is a reference to the world of complaint, of no chance, of "It can't be done," of "It's too difficult," of "The resources are not there," of "Others do it better," of "It's hopeless." This is one type of dialogue or conversation. The other world is one of *radiating possibilities*, in which possibilities flow in every direction. This is a world where we cannot see the end result, but still believe a good one is out there: "In the measurement world, you set a goal and strive for it. In the universe of possibility, you set the context and let life unfold."[41]

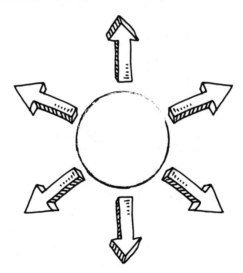

---

40   *Link:* https://vimeo.com/18625943

41   Zander, Ben: *The Art of Possibility: Transforming Professional and Personal Life*, Penguin, 2002

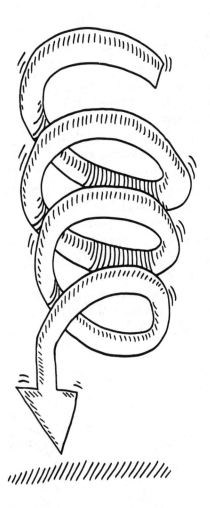

Zander's two types of conversations

These two worlds represent two different conversations. We have all experienced *downward spiral* conversations where someone makes a negative comment that triggers a huge gravitational pull, creating a downward vortex that sucks in everyone around them. For some reason, these conversations are hard to resist.

The other conversation is one of possibility where the arrows go out in all directions; it is a conversation where people

158

are inspired by possibilities, where opportunities rule the day. These conversations can also draw people in.

The world you live in and the conversations you have is a choice. Your task in *Live with Intent* is to break out of downward spirals or avoid them altogether. Think of possibility, and choose to live in the world of possibility. Choose your conversations with intent.

Zander "A" Student

One of Benjamin Zander's secrets for inspiring performance is a unique approach to grading. He discovered many students are held back in their expressive life by internal voices of self-doubt: "Others play better than you do," or "You are going to miss that difficult note."

To help students overcome their fears and self-doubts, he has them write him a letter at the start of the school year. The letter begins: "Dear Mr. Zander, I got an A because..." The students then describe who they will become as a result of his class.

Zander personally reads each letter and internalizes the person the student wants to become and then teaches and coaches the person that the student will become. More often than not, students become the person they aspire to in their letters.

We invite you to write yourself a letter, generously describing the person you will become as a student of *Live with Intent*. Be bold. Be specific. Be your biggest fan and advocate. We would be delighted to read your letters.

Resonance

Good listening and dialogue skills can lead to almost magical relationship results. The principle is simple: ***Only to the extent that your counterpart feels heard and understood about his concerns will he or she believe that you have the competence to add value.*** You can actively build confidence and gain influence by using the principles of general reliability and honesty.

TIP

SEE—Reflect on where you are today. Who have you inspired with your words? Who has inspired you with his/her words? Where are you most successful in using language to create your desired reality? When is communication and listening hard for you? Are there words you would like to take back and apologize for? What are the biggest barriers for you for mutual understanding?

DO

A. Eye contact

Pay attention to the expression of your eyes—they are the mirror of your soul. Make an effort to bring openness into your expression. A fixed, unwavering gaze always makes an impression on your partner, especially if you talk face to face with him or her. Acquire a solid and open-eye contact and hold the contact—each time a little bit more.

B. Expression

Check your facial expression from time to time or have someone video you while you tell or explain something. Look closely to see what impression you make on yourself. Is the impression one that you want to convey? Your facial expressions will either enhance or detract from your messages. Great speakers train and rehearse in front of the mirror. Get to know your expressions. The power that you need for future success will emanate from this image.

C. Speak in the correct past tense

Say out loud the following sentences in the different past tenses and feel the effect they have on your body:

"I have been tired."	*"I was tired."*
"I have been frustrated."	*"I was frustrated."*
"I have been ill."	*"I was ill."*
"I have been sad."	*"I was sad."*

Past tense: Perfect	*Past tense: Imperfect*
◦ *Stirs up feelings.* ◦ *The perfect tense denotes an action that is completed in the past, however its consequences / or results reach into the present and still have meaning.* ◦ *For the repetition of experiences or events that are to be presented in a colorful and lively manner.* ◦ *Helps to create common ground.* ◦ *Relaxes communication, builds bridges to customers, children, and patients, etc.*	◦ *Is factual, complete and allows serenity.* ◦ *The past tense indicates that past events are complete. It is the so-called narrative tense and also designates unspoken thoughts (narrated monologue).*

D. Remove the subjunctive

Remove the subjunctive in all aspects and you will have new relationships—with the same people! You just need to cut out:

We would…

We would have to…

We should…

and bring into your relationships: We *will*…

Talk in a decisive way. Many people do this at work very well; now remove the subjunctive from the language that you use at home.

E. Formulate new "I must" sentences in the future tense

Write 10 "I must/have to" sentences that you often say to yourself.

Now rewrite each sentence using the future tense.

For example:

Have to/must: *"I have to write that offer."*

Future: *"I will write that offer this afternoon."*

Rewriting statements in future tense takes away the pressure and gives you more structure. Feeling more proactive will increase your performance enormously. This is achieved by using the correct choice of language (which creates a reality and brings results). Stay on the ball! Turn all of your "have to" statements into the future and couple them with a time frame.

F. Remove all negative formulations

Upon reflection, it is sometimes shocking to find just how many unnecessary negative formulations[42] we use in our daily language. Remove this from your language completely:

---

42 According to ST Brown, the negative formulation which is used to express positive thought or actions comes out of an emotional uncertainty, or out of fear of injury or the possibility of criticism. [...] As such, the person speaking has left open the option that he or she did not mean what was said, just in case the other party does not react the way that person had hoped or expected. (p. 81, line 21ff.)

Negative format	Positive format
"I am not unhappy with my husband."	"I am happy with my husband."
"I'm not doing poorly."	"I'm doing well."
"Why not?"	"Yes, ok!"
"I can't complain."	"It is going well."
"The food wasn't bad."	"The food tasted good."
"The project results were not unsatisfactory."	"I was satisfied with the results."
"Our team is not the worst."	"Our team has potential for improvement."
"Oh no!"	"That has affected me."

Negative formulations ensure that you debilitate yourself and those around you; they suck out energy instead of infusing power and energy. Make it easy for yourself and the people you live and work with—rigorously reject negative formulations!

G. Remove double negatives

It wasn't uninteresting.

I cannot say that I do not disagree with you (a quip by Groucho Marx).

He was not incompetent. She is not unattractive.

It's not unusual to be loved by anyone.

I have so much to do that I haven't ever got time to rest.

Her daughters seldom ever visit her at the hospital.
I didn't do nothing.
The pilot could not find nowhere to land.
I barely got any sleep last night. I don't have no money for the movie.

H. Stop gossiping!

Gossip is a matter of choice and attitude. From now on, decide to be loyal to the absent person, since "gossiping is the first of all vices." Everybody involved in the discussion will hear you and remember that you were loyal and spoke well of the absent individual. You reacted as if he or she was in the room with you. Especially in a professional setting, people will remember this well, because they know that in the next discussion they might be the individual who is absent. Loyalty to the absent generates trust and healthy relationships. It is a powerful application of the communication principle. If you constantly apply these principles, you will take an enormous step forward in relation to character and competence.

I. Important principles
- Use a clear and concise sentence structure.
- Speak calmly and slowly. Avoid "swallowing" the end syllables.
- Give clear instructions, and ask questions with clarity.
- Make small *pauses* at the end of a sentence—this increases the effect of statements!
- Pay attention to your posture and your tone vibration—your body communicates automatically to others.
- Convince your customers with authentic facial expressions, body language and gestures.
- Formulate clear requests or concerns.

J. Practice respectful language and conversations—the family piggy bank

The family piggy bank exercise is an exciting opportunity for your family. Every family member has a piggy bank with a beginning sum of 3 euros or 3 U.S. dollars. For example, when the parents notice that respectful words are used, the piggy bank receives 25 or 50 cents. When there is disharmony in the family and no respect in the communication, the disrespectful person has to pay 10 cents. Design the exercise as a thrilling game, full of fun, and it could become one of the best recurring educational activities in your family.

K. Take the word "one" out of your vocabulary ("One always speaks of oneself...")

We live in an age when language is being reduced to acronyms (e.g. LOL), abbreviations, icons, and slang. When we speak with clear and precise language, we convey our thoughts and feelings more clearly. Next time you watch a talk show or interview on TV, notice when the person who is being interviewed starts to speak about himself and when he lapses into the "one" or "some" form of speech to continue reciting his experiences, instead of the "I" form. Often when people speak about emotions and feelings, the "one" starts to appear: "One has to be careful that..." or "Some have seen that...," etc.

We suggest that you always use the "I" form. Why? As long as I am talking about myself I have a connection to what I am saying. I hear that I am talking about myself, and I can be in touch with my inner feelings. I am consciously aware of the importance of what I say. I can feel that all that I share about myself has a direct connection to me. Hence, I will behave differently than a person who speaks of "one" when talking about himself. Such a person won't find the strength and motivation to seek long-term solutions for his life. He won't be able to "access" himself and know where he really stands on things. This creates a long-term incapacity. If he does not show up as a concrete person in a conversation, even when he is talking about *himself*, then he makes no personal connection with anyone else. He only bores himself and others.

Exercise: In your next conversations with friends, declare "one" to be a taboo word. Everyone should notice this word. If they say it, then they need to repeat the whole sentence.

GROW—The following *checklist* will help you track your growth:
- Practice active, empathic listening.
- Try first to understand your counterpart, then talk. "Speech is silver, but silence is golden".
- Try to hold eye-contact during conversations.
- Present open and friendly facial expressions.
- Make sure to use the right past tense, the simple present.
- Remove the subjunctive from your vocabulary and replace it with the future tense.
- Transform "I must" sentences into "I will" sentences.
- Remove negative formulations and double negatives.
- Stop gossiping.
- Follow the principles of correct articulation of your thoughts and feelings.
- Remove the word "one" from your vocabulary.

Use every exercise for two to three days and work at least two to three weeks on this chapter.

Affirmations
- You engage in active, empathic listening.
- You try first to understand others and then talk clearly to be understood.
- You maintain eye contact during conversations.
- You present open and friendly facial expressions.
- You use the right verb tenses.
- You transform "I must" sentences into "I will" sentences.
- You remove negative formulations and double negatives.
- You never gossip.
- You articulate honestly your thoughts and feelings.

CHAPTER 8
AUTOSUGGESTION

TAP INTO
FRESH POWER

YOUR **WORST ENEMY** CANNOT HARM YOU AS MUCH AS YOUR OWN UNGUARDED **THOUGHTS**. NOT EVEN YOUR MOTHER, YOUR FATHER OR ANY OTHER LIKEMINDED PERSON CAN DO YOU AS MUCH **GOOD AS YOUR OWN** CORRECT, **SELF-CONTROLLED** THOUGHT.

BUDDHA

The **TREASURES** that are still hidden inside the earth **far exceed** the assets of all the investors, investment bankers, high finance and stock exchanges in the world. Geologists claim that all the gold that is circulating in the world and all the diamonds in jewelry shops and vaults—all the jewelry that sparkles in the shop windows and from the necks of wealthy people—are mere trinkets compared to what still lies hidden in the earth.

Likewise, the treasures that **remain hidden in our MINDS** far exceed what we have expressed so far. Our daily activity with its "full consciousness" does not allow us to unlock the **INVISIBLE yet powerful activity** of our subconscious. When we realize how unconditional and powerful our subconscious is and how it works, we stand in awe of the **HUGE opportunities that await us.** Only the tip of an iceberg is above water; by far the largest part is underwater—invisible. In like manner, only the tip of our **KNOWLEDGE** is visible or conscious. **We are aware only of a small portion of it.** The largest part of it is hidden in the depths of our unconscious, and most of what controls and directs us is **our subconscious.** The subconscious is more powerful than the conscious because it controls most of our life processes and actions. Throughout our life it stores all the important information. However, this data is not directly accessible to our consciousness. **We are not aware of its content—it is hidden in the DEPTHS of our mind.**

"The subconscious wins ... every time"[43] The winner in the conflict between the conscious and subconscious is always the subconscious because it controls most processes of life that are not directly accessible to us. Therefore, connect yourself with your subconscious mind. Learn by *autosuggestion* how you can actively change the ways and beliefs of your subconscious mind step by step! If we change the beliefs within us, we can control our destiny.

The key lies in our words and thoughts! The words and thoughts anchored within us have extraordinary potential power. The more we think a thought, the more we speak a word, the more its content becomes part of our reality and part of ourselves. And the more this thought is a part of us, the more it can create and change our lives.

Our conviction produces our experience; our experience produces our belief.

Our perception depends on our convictions. Our perceptions confirm our beliefs. Our beliefs influence our perceptions, thereby creating over and above their own reality.

As long as our beliefs inform us that we are good, lovable and valuable, then this dynamic will not end—we will continue to be assured of the attention of others and be convinced that success is possible; after all, we "know" that we deserve all that we have.

However, when our inner patterns sound like "I cannot do it," "I am worthless" or "Others can always see everything better than I can," we will struggle in our work and relationships. Sadly, such negative, strength-stealing convictions are common for many people. Therefore, we need to replace them with other beliefs that give us permission to have success and that actually enable our success.

---

43 Bandler, R., Grindler, M., *Metasprache und Psychotherapie*, Junfermann Verlag, 2005

Two Examples of the Power of Belief

The unconditional nature of this psychological law of belief is evident in two examples.

The first example shows the effect of the mind's eye images—a variation of the inner beliefs. Imagine that there is a one-meter wide board lying in front of you on the floor. It has a length of 20 meters. Run on the board for the full 20 meters. Stride across the board for its entire length. You do that with ease. This is an easy exercise.

Now, imagine that someone blindfolds you, takes you to another place, presents a similar board and asks you to run on this board for 20 meters. For better orientation, you are given a taut rope to hold onto. You may feel discomfort, the feeling of having to be extra careful; therefore, you move ahead very carefully and slowly. But not a big problem—the experiment is a success! Now, you take off the blindfold and see with horror that you have walked along a one-meter-wide board across a gap that is 100 meters above the ground.

If someone would require you to go that way again, you would vehemently refuse for fear of falling from 100 meters. In fact, you might be incapable of taking even three steps on this boardwalk without falling into the abyss. Why? Because imagining the danger of falling from this height would make failure even more likely.

As long as the board is on the floor, you see no danger in running across it. You feel in full possession of your skills; therefore, you are in full possession of your abilities. Children regularly do reckless things, hopefully without incident, because they are not fully aware of the danger. Hence, they proceed with confidence. However, as an adult, you have sufficient experience to know, that if you tumble 100 meters, the best you can expect are shattered limbs! The idea that you could fall into the abyss overcomes you and paralyzes you. In a second attempt, your thoughts would likely cause you to fall and fail.

In the second example, imagine you have a juicy lemon in front of you. You take this juicy lemon in your hand and smell it. Through the peel, you can already smell the tartness. Now in your imagination, cut the yellow lemon in half. The lemon juice runs out. You take one half in your hand and smell it again—you can smell the sourness much more clearly. Now take an imaginary large bite of the lemon.

If you have visually pictured this thought, then you will have noted two things: 1) Your saliva has increased; and 2) your face has recoiled.

This small thought experiment highlights two interesting aspects:

Thoughts and fantasies are forces that cause your body to react. The body and its facial muscles react as if you had actually bitten into a lemon. You felt the same way, as you would have if you had done it. The truth is that every thought and idea, whether positive or negative, has an impact on your mental and physical being.

The brain cannot distinguish whether it is actually experiencing something or whether it is an illusion. Although you know that this example was only in your imagination, for your brain it was real. The brain carries out its work systematically, almost like a computer, not caring whether something is real or imaginary. It processes any information as if it was real. In computer terms, they say: *garbage in, garbage out*, meaning if you input rubbish, all you will get back is rubbish.

> *"In order to steer the imagination, only two things are necessary: first you have to know (and only a few know this) that such a thing is possible; and secondly, you must know the means by which it is accomplished. This method is very simple. Even without meaning to, from the very first day of our life we have been applying this method from the dark corners of our subconscious daily. Unfortunately, if applied incorrectly it is quite often damaging. This method is called autosuggestion."*
> ~ *Émile Coué, Father and Pioneer of Autosuggestion (1857–1926)*

Whether it relates to thoughts, behavior patterns, conditioning or trauma, we have a powerful medicine of autosuggestion as an antidote against these limitations. Instead of preventing us from achieving our goal, we can, with the correct application, use autosuggestion to "overwrite" deep beliefs we have of ourselves.

Because autosuggestion changes our imagination, it affects our attitudes and our actions and ultimately changes our destiny. It will strengthen you where you now have deficits. It can be the puzzle piece needed to complete the full picture.

The four laws of Émile Coué:
1. In the conflict between intention and imagination, imagination invariably wins.
2. In the conflict between intention and imagination, the imagination has as much weight and influence as the willpower times square.
3. When intention and imagination are combined, they do not add up—they multiply both energies.
4. Imagination is steerable, meaning you can direct its course.

Autosuggestion acts directly on our minds and not on material matters. It gives our subconscious the messages we choose. The subconscious understands these messages as an invitation, which it fulfils. It will then ensure that you get what you desire. Hence, when applied correctly, autosuggestion makes us masters of ourselves and our destiny!

Thomas: In 1988 Carsten Maschmeyer founded the financial services company Allgemeiner Wirtschaftsdienst, better known as AWD. The company was publicly listed on the German stock exchange in 2000 and bought by Swiss Life in 2007 for 1.2 billion euros. [44]

While successful, Maschmeyer polarizes like no other entrepreneur in Germany. When he was featured on the cover

---

44   See www.spiegel.de, *AWD-Gründer: Carsten Maschmeyer verlässt Swiss Life*, http://www.spiegel.de/wirtschaft/unternehmen/awd-gruender-carsten-maschmeyer-verlaesst-swiss-life-a-802373.html, 12/07/2011, accessed on 08/27/2015

of *Manager Magazin* in September 2015, the caption below his picture reads: *"Gross, Mann, Sucht. Carsten Maschmeyer Der Selfmademilliardär gibt gern den smarten Superfinanzier. Ist er aber nicht"*[45] (in English: Craving for status. The self-made billionaire likes to present himself as a smart super-financier. In fact, he isn't). The article focused on Maschmeyer's company's losses, which totaled fewer than 10 million euros.[46]

Likewise, on many other topics, Carsten Maschmeyer has often been attacked by the press; the business media regularly look for the next scandal involving him. However, I consider this question to be much more exciting: "How has Carsten become the man he is today?" In my opinion his development from a child from a modest background to a highly successful entrepreneur is the truly remarkable story.

He provides the answer to this question in his book *Selfmade: erfolg reich leben* (in English: Selfmade: how to live rich and successful). In this book, he devotes an entire chapter to this mindset we call autosuggestion, and his ideas mirror our ideas on this fundamental principle. He says, "With your thoughts you decide what you pour into the mold of your life. Firmly believe in yourself. Think outside the box and leave old thought patterns behind you. Look forward to new horizons of thoughts, to great insights that will open up great prospects. Your best friend is your subconscious. Align your subconscious mind to success, around the clock, seven days a week, 24 hours a day. Often a difficult situation is just a reflection of your state of mind."[47]

Success is a question of attitude. Carsten Maschmeyer clearly shows with his autosuggestion titled "Success" the positive benefits of autosuggestion.

45   Maier, A., *Gross, Mann, Sucht. Carsten Maschmeyer Der Selfmademilliardär gibt gern den smarten Superfinanzier. Ist er aber nicht*, in Manager Magazin 09/2015, p. 8ff.

46   See Maier, A., *Gross, Mann, Sucht. Carsten Maschmeyer Der Selfmademilliardär gibt gern den smarten Superfinanzier. Ist er aber nicht*, in Manager Magazin 09/2015, p. 8ff.

47   Maschmeyer, C., *Selfmade. erfolg reich leben*, 4th edition, Ariston, 2012, p. 186ff.

To achieve the best results with autosuggestion, follow 10 guidelines:

1. Have in your mind a clear picture of the person you want to be. Try to get the clearest and most positive and vibrant image of this person. What are his or her special features? What can he or she do particularly well? What sets him or her apart? Where will he or she be?

2. Write this visualization of your autosuggestion in your learning diary in simple sentences in the "you" form. For example: "*You* are strong," "*You* can do it" or "*You* are attractive." Use only positive statements. The brain cannot process the word "*not*" and acts as if it did not exist. If you say: "*You do not want to smoke anymore*," the brain processes only the statement "*You smoke more*," and the mind's eye pictures you smoking more!

3. Formulate a sentence of about 15 to 20 words that expresses the conviction that what you wish to happen has already taken place. The sentence is in the present tense and assumes that you already have all the necessary talents needed to execute this visualization.

4. Give this sentence a positive form (see examples below), thus reaffirming your confidence in good, speedy results. Never mention your mistakes, not even to express that you will eliminate them (see negative examples below). To do so would only anchor those negative mistakes more! For example: "I passed my high school exam and am studying my chosen subject."

5. Autosuggestion is more than just an exercise for the mind. Yes, you have to keep repeating the formula, but the constant repetition of autosuggestion—when carried out with pleasure and calmness—enables you to accept the autosuggestion and internalize it deep inside. Undertake these exercises with a calm attitude and in good spirits. For even stronger results, harness your emotions and a positive mental attitude behind the autosuggestion.

6. Choose to believe that your desires are possible.

7. Use autosuggestion at night before you fall asleep, and repeat it during the night if you happen to wake up; use it an additional two or three times during the day. Go over it during

moments of relaxation and whenever you are preparing for or are facing difficulties.

8. During these exercises, have a specific goal in mind: for example, acquiring a specific ability. You need to work persistently until you achieve the final result.

9. Incorporate the autosuggestion formula into three daily five-minute to fifteen-minute walks until by every long step you automatically think about your autosuggestion. Repeat the formula constantly and continuously, so that it reaches deeper into your subconscious mind.

10. Do not be surprised if you experience an increase in the number of "strange coincidences" or moments of serendipity that fall into your hands.

Possible Sources of Error

You may not achieve the results you expect from autosuggestion for any of four reasons:

- We give up too early and are not patient enough in the application. Success cannot be seriously expected after only a few days—only after consistent repetition for several weeks will the desired effect start to appear.
- Sometimes we are not aware of what we can achieve with the autosuggestion. Do not expect to see too much in the short term and too little in the long term. This method cannot pick the stars from heaven for us, but it will impact your bank account directly.
- Maybe your wishes were too big or too generally formulated. For example: "I'm rich and sought after."
- You lack trust, real intent, firm decision and deep faith. Tell yourself over and over again, that things are already better *now*, not that they "will be better tomorrow." Tell yourself that you are moving forward, even though it may be in small steps. Always choose to think that *anything is possible*! A positive mental attitude is the sensible option, and you can and should trust these thought patterns. Soon, the first successes will be visible and they will give you the motivation and courage to press on!

Please note that a new formula can only replace the old (consciously or unconsciously) if the feeling that triggers it is better or more pleasant than the one that caused the old conviction. Therefore, your emotions may be the best guides. When you say your autosuggestion formula, make sure that you also "feel" it. If your feelings change towards being comfortable (cozy, open, free, large, and warm), the affirmation is the correct one. If there is no such feeling or if your affirmation clearly does not feel pleasant, you need to reconsider the sentence or the desired characteristic. You should never work against your feelings.

Your subconscious mind has greater power than your willpower, and you need to harness both of these resources equally. In order to find out if there is an internal resistance against the contents of your formula, it is helpful to change the formula from the "you" form into the "I" form, as follows:

- I want to be ... successful
- I can be ... successful
- I am allowed to be ... successful
- I deserve to be ... successful

Speak these sentences out loud and feel what is happening to you. If you do not respond completely positively to the sentences, try converting the autosuggestion back to the "you" form and saying it again that way. Internal resistance can manifest itself in many different ways. For example: You could find the sentences ridiculous or the exercise completely unnecessary; your neck suddenly itches; you have to cough or swallow; or perhaps you have some other physical reaction. If this occurs, then it is better to change the sentences.

Continue to do this until you have a warm and pleasant feeling. It could be that the content has to be diluted; for example, you might need to go from "I am worthy" to "I am okay." It will only work when it feels right for you! We recommend to use the "you" form instead of the "I" form. The "you" form has a stronger influence on our subconscious and is a stronger command, and less of a reflective mode which the "I" form is often in the self-talk we use. Therefore be sure to use the "you" form.

The autosuggestion formulas will strengthen you, and your desires will begin to grow, gain strength and become indispensable on your path to effectiveness and success. Stay positive in the continuous execution of the autosuggestion, even when progress is slow initially. Eventually progress will certainly kick in! And the successes that you notice will give you the courage to continue and expand the autosuggestion.

TIP

SEE

Prepare a list of characteristics that reflect how you want to see yourself.

DO

Now formulate an affirmation with the characteristics that you consider the most important and urgent into an autosuggestion formula. Make sure it includes the previously listed characteristics ("you" form, present tense, positive words).

Write the sentence on a small piece of paper and put it in your wallet or in your calendar. Place the sentence in different areas of your apartment. If you do not want it read by others, find a symbol that represents the sentence. Strive every day to say this sentence out loud as often as possible and continually practice the methods that have been given previously.

Here are some examples of autosuggestion formulas:

Positive example	Negative example
You are healthy and strong and master every challenge.	You are not ill and not tired.
You live in London and have the right job.	You live in London and do not have to fight to survive.
You are self-confident and strong. You exude confidence and clarity.	You do not have a problem with self-confidence. You do not appear to be chaotic.
You are independent and confident.	You are not dependent on others.
You feel free and powerful.	You are not bound by others or ... anymore.

GROW

Your personal autosuggestion formula is your affirmation for this chapter. This plus the checklist below will accelerate your growth.

Create your formula

Create your autosuggestion formula according to the following aspects:
- Imagine a clear image of the person you want to become.
- Make simple sentences.
- Write your sentence as if your aim has already been achieved.
- Only name positive attributes.
- Repeat your autosuggestion in a calm, positive and relaxed environment.

- Believe in the fulfilment of your wish.
- Bring your autosuggestion to your mind several times a day.
- Stay on target until you have achieved your goal.
- Implement daily autosuggestion walks in your weekly schedule.

Checklist

1. Accept and use the power of autosuggestion.
2. Revise your autosuggestion formula if you don't feel good with it.
3. Integrate your autosuggestion formula in your daily life.
4. Integrate five or six times each day when you practice and improve autosuggestion.

Part 3

How You Will Get There

TOOLS FOR YOUR PATH AHEAD

In this third part, we explore the question, "How you will get there?", and introduce four foundational principles: Intent, Abundance, Synergy and Preparation for Crisis.

CHAPTER 9

Be Intentional: Reaching your horizon

CHAPTER 10

Be Abundant: Inviting others to your horizon

CHAPTER 11

Go Exponential: Seeking energy

CHAPTER 12

Prepare for Crisis: Walking beyond the runway

THE MOST DIFFICULT THING IS THE DECISION TO ACT, THE REST IS MERELY TENACITY

~Amelia Earhart

CHAPTER 9
BE INTENTIONAL

REACHING
YOUR HORIZON

IF THERE IS A 'SECRET' TO EFFECTIVENESS, IT IS CONCENTRATION", WROTE PETER DRUCKER[48] IN 1966. The internationally acclaimed founder of modern management theory postulates that the need for concentration is rooted in human nature. He describes the secret of those who do so many different types of tasks without too much stress this way:

"They plan a certain time to achieve just one thing. By doing this, they achieve, in end effect, the fact that they spend much less time doing things than the rest of us."[49]

This means that today's **multitasking** (doing several things at the same time) is actually **counterproductive** to effectiveness.

Peter Drucker shows that **BEING INTENTIONAL** about doing **one thing at a time** is kinder to the practitioner and leads to faster goal achievement.

---

[48] Drucker, Peter F., *The Effective Executive*, Harper & Row, New York, 1966

[49] Drucker, Peter F., *The Ideal Leadership*, Econ Publishing, Düsseldorf, 1995, p. 161

In some situations, ***concentration on one thing*** is obvious. For example, when a pilot takes the airplane into descent on the final phase of an approach, he prepares for the most intensive part of the flight—the landing. The weather is checked, wind direction known, navigation set, the landing method is mentally rehearsed, the radio frequencies are engaged, the passengers briefed, the maps ready and details for an emergency landing are in the hands and head. Every detail begins to be important!

On the final approach, just before landing, only one thing applies—concentration! Various things can happen, but the professional pilot never neglects his most important assignment—making a safe landing. When approaching the ground, he pays meticulous attention to the speed, height and direction of the plane. In that moment, many other things are absolutely irrelevant and an automatic "No!" is a frequent response. From experience, his crew knows that in this situation absolute concentration is required and any distraction that does not serve the cause won't be tolerated. He is intentionally working with discipline and professionalism. The pilot is neither rude nor authoritarian, but completely focused on carrying out his duty.

Likewise, an effective businessman is not rude, authoritarian or egocentric when he decides to be intentional about focusing on solving the most important issue at hand.

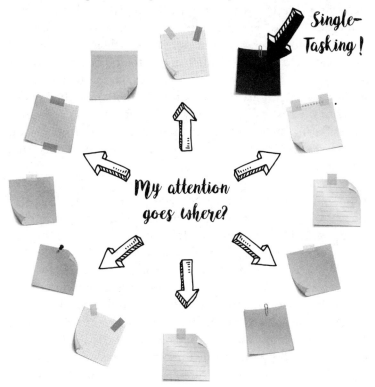

This should be our procedure! Our daily routines must be intentionally carried out in a concentrated manner. But, in order for us to get to the right point in the next phase we need to have a general overview; we need to decide on the most important thing to focus on and then have the dedication to follow through on it.

With concentration, you can achieve your objectives in much less time!

Being intentional about the topics you focus on saves you time because you don't need to keep "ramping up" to get back into the subject. Getting back into the details of any task is very time-consuming. In industry and in manual labor we call this "set-up time," and we save much time and emotional energy if we do not have to do it repeatedly.

To work steadily on one thing does not mean: to work without breaks, to work in a hurry or to rush yourself. Such habits lead to inferior results, decreased effectiveness and poor quality.

Although having a positive attitude helps us to excel in our workflow, we still often fall into the traps of *urgency* and *overtime*. Whether it is a compulsion for perfection or another underlying pattern, we can often no longer distinguish between what is really necessary and what is not. However, by concentrating and focusing on that which is most important, we can accomplish our obligations and have time for other activities.

Consider the example of **Sheryl Sandberg**. Success runs through her life like a thread. She was the best-paid manager in Silicon Valley as COO with an annual income of $30 million dollars in 2011. Following the IPO of Facebook in 2012, her fortune is estimated to be worth at least $2.7 billion dollars.

No one achieves such success without power, effectiveness and focus. It looks like she has a clear idea about what comes first in her life: The strong family bond influences her daily. She resists the widespread madness that one must work around the clock to be successful in Silicon Valley. "Every evening I go home at 5:30 p.m. to eat dinner with the kids," she says. "It depends on what you accomplish, not on how long you're there." That is easy to say, but for most of us not easy to do.

> *"There are always more productive things to do tomorrow than the time in which to perform them, and more favorable opportunities than capable people who can execute them—not to mention the abundance of arising problems and crises. One must therefore make a decision, which of the tasks you want to*

give priority and which are believed to be less important. The only question is who makes the decision—the executive himself or an urgency which is influencing him."

~ Peter Drucker

One thing is sure: ***Tomorrow you will have 24 hours less to live: tomorrow the duration of your life will be exactly 24 hours shorter!*** This should be enough motivation to make something out of today, because you can't bring it back. Therefore, make today count! Tomorrow, this day (today) will stand in the past and will have influenced the future. Life is like sand flowing through our hands. Do not waste resources—time, strength, money, relationships, energy, or fortitude. You may be tempted to think that you can make up for lost time and opportunity later, but lost time is irretrievable!

"There is no greater harm than that of time wasted."

~ Michelangelo

This chapter shows you how to be intentional as you divide your time wisely and do justice to what is important in your life. You need to fearlessly implement these principles:
- Select the future rather than the past.
- Concentrate more on opportunities than problems.
- Choose your own direction, rather than drift with the crowd.
- Set your sights high and strive for new results instead of seeking only for safety and easy success ("low-hanging-fruit").
- Don't be influenced by your mistakes, but learn from them—let go and then move on.
- Be able to say "No" and not be swayed.

TIP

SEE

Look for the activities and projects that tangibly advance you toward your horizon. Ask yourself questions such as: *"If I had not started this or that project, would I start it again?"* or *"Is this activity getting me closer to my horizon?"*

DO

A. Let go of yesterday and be intentional about today.

Stop the activity or greatly reduce your commitment to it if your answer is not an unconditional "Yes."

B. Concentrate work in block hours.

Obtain a stopwatch with an audible signal and set it for 50 minutes. When you are working or planning to devote time to something, train your mind to stay concentrated and focused until the signal sounds. Do not allow yourself to be distracted or interrupted. Inform those around you that you do not want to be disturbed for the next 50 minutes. Those around you will then support you instead of interrupting you.

This principle alone can double your effectiveness. When the 50 minutes are up, take a short break of about 10 minutes. Drink some water, breathe fresh air if possible and move around! Thus fortified, you create the best conditions to go into a good productive block for the next hour. See for yourself what happens when you perform two or more block hours per day.

To boost your productivity, implement this method of activity today. Whether you are self-employed, an employee or a student, you can increase your impact dramatically by applying the block hour. *You then do in the block hour exactly what you get paid to do!* This is, even in organizations, a rarity!

Know how to prioritize your time. Don't suppose the attending to *urgent matters* first will afford you time later for *important matters*. The autopilot response to urgent matters will automatically expand, decreasing your strength, effectiveness and motivation. Urgent tasks should not necessarily be done first. Often, doing the more important things first is more effective. So, try taking care of *important matters* first, and then taking care of all the so-called urgent matters. As every effective person knows, important matters should never be at the mercy of urgent matters.

If you habitually attend to important matters (relationships, education, family) only after accomplishing all of the urgent tasks, at some point you will experience some major challenges. The important activities must never become dependent upon the completion of the urgent things in your life. If you devote time to important matters only after completing urgent matters, you will never have enough time—the day, week, month or year will always end too soon.

So, start with what is important—do the important things first. Know what *first* means to you, and make it visible in your everyday life.

C. Weekly planning.

> *"Use well your time, so rapidly it flies; Method will teach*
> *you time to win."*
> ~ *Goethe in Faust*

First, understand that checklists with A, B, C priorities, lists or documents that you execute purely in a chronological order are outdated. Today's dynamic demands on your life call for a more effective method. We believe that *the key to meeting all challenges in time management is to divide and plan your life roles within a weekly framework.* Within the seven-day timeframe of one week, you can map out all areas of your life. If you can't plan all areas in that week, you will find it difficult or impossible to plan every month and quarter. Let the week be your personal project. Start every week from today with a compass, the result of a principle-based weekly planning session.

Here are five steps for being intentional in weekly planning:

Step 1: Review your goals, priorities, life motto and mission.
Take some time, put on some music and make a pot of tea
while you organize. Then tackle your big issues, consider your
goals and review your goal collage. In this step, you personally
connect your heart and emotions with your goals and life
purpose. You are now working with a different perspective—
it's about your life, not just next week's activities. It's about how
the next week will help you achieve your goals. What should
you keep, support, develop, make new or do? How can you use
the time you have next week to align your life to your goals,
priorities and mission? What long-term goals do you have
in your various roles? What legacy do you want to leave as a
parent or child? For this purpose, we find it helpful to write a
description of the legacy you wish to leave behind in each role
(see Step 2 in the table in point B).

*Step 2: Classify the seven roles of your personal and
professional life, and set aside time to perform each role.* The
seven roles in your life represent your main responsibilities and
relationships—areas in both your personal and professional
life. These roles might include: husband/wife; father/mother;
son/daughter; sister/brother; friend; club member; student;
product manager; researcher; HR manager; employee. For each
role, write down how you would like other people to remember
you. Write down the good things others might say about you,
such as how your partner sees you in the relationship. You are
trying to assess what "footprints in the sand" or legacy you will
leave behind through your actions and attitude. Now, decide
what activities you need to plan for in this next week to meet
your goals in your various roles. Remember to attend first to the
important matters, not the urgent ones. What will you do in
order to get closer to achieving your goals in each of your roles?
Specify a day and time for making progress toward your goals.
Set an appointment with yourself to plan what is important in
your life. For example, you might build the weekly structure as
follows:

No.	Role (a)	Legacy (b)	Weekly Plan (c)	Calendar (d)
1	Profession, career, earnings	He is among the top three performers in the company. His results are professional and high quality. This year he received the performance bonus.	Closure with customer xyz	Tuesday 10 a.m. to 2 p.m.
2	Family, private life	She is the backbone of strength for her partner and children. Her family is a place of strength and inspiration for all family members.	Special outing on Saturday	Saturday – all day. Preparation on Wednesday evening.
3	Couple, marriage, partner	He enjoys a remarkably deep and romantic relationship. He takes time to listen, which results in a deep mutual understanding.	Go on a special date together and make time to listen	Friday from 6 p.m. onwards
4	Learning, growth, development	She is constantly learning. She invests in development and growth.	Live with Intent, read Chapter 4	Sunday from 3 to 5 p.m.
5	Product manager	The product development of our team will significantly influence the success of the company. We are a modern and innovative team.	New development, international research	Tuesday 10 a.m. until noon
6	Friend, networking	She is a true friend. She is surrounded by good and reliable people who value her.	Visit Klaus	Monday evening
7	Spiritual development, church	He is a value-oriented and spiritually mature person.	Meditation and scripture study	Daily

Step 3: Reflect on and evaluate the previous week. Look at the last week's calendar and compass, your guiding document and the product of your weekly planning session. Evaluate how the week went. Recognize positive and inhibitory patterns. Each week ask yourself these questions: What went really well? What am I proud of, what do I want to keep? Have I set the right priorities? Am I happy with the results? Have I used the time to achieve my goals? What stopped me from

accomplishing my plans? Which unachieved goals do I want to accomplish this week? Have I neglected any roles or goals? Do I need to define a new role? What legacy do I want to leave within the individual roles? Do I devote enough attention to each role? What do I feel is more important to me than what I am showing by my actions? Do I recognize and express appreciation for all those who support me and keep me going? Am I attending first to important, not urgent, matters?

Step 4: Set goals for each role. At the start of the week, set only *one* goal per role that is important to you. This way you can better focus on the *important* activities. You might ask yourself, for example: "What is the one goal in the role of 'being a mother' which would create a real difference this week?" In the weekly schedule, you also include other tasks you want to accomplish; but in the weekly planning session, you first identify only one important goal per role. In this way you always have on your mind what this week's most important goal is in each role. The remaining activities, projects and tasks will surely fill out your planning system quickly. The essential things must not get lost. That's why you have the compass with your roles and major goals for the week.

As you do the weekly planning, set a weekly target for all your roles, with a maximum of seven. This keeps your overall goals and priorities in perspective. Now, note these goals and designate a specific time and day for each of these seven objectives/priorities/appointments for the coming week to ensure they get your attention and don't become victims of urgent tasks. Use the Weekly Compass checklist to connect your roles, weekly targets and dates on a form. You can integrate these principles into each planning system, either analog or digital. You can obtain these forms from the website of Reichart Effectiveness Consulting (www.reichart.biz).

Step 5: Weekly organization. Planning and organizing your week gives you a clear view on your life and helps you to consistently focus on the important issues. Just looking at the daily schedule is not enough as it has a too limited view of the important issues. For example, when a working mother finds herself in a stressful situation, she will generally only concentrate on the urgent tasks in her daily plan. However, in the proposed role model we give names to the important areas and people in our lives. After all, they give our lives meaning, structure and stability. Therefore, organize yourself with a weekly routine and rhythm.

GROW

Affirmations
The following affirmations will accelerate your growth.
- You are intentional in the way you invest your time and energy.
- You are focused on your goal and are progressing step by step in the right direction.
- You dedicate yourself to the correct topics.
- Through your dedication and focus you develop great strength.
- You have enough time every week to set your weekly compass.
- Your compass directs you to your true horizon.
- You can take care of the key topics in your life.
- You create lasting solutions.
- You deepen the relationships that are important to you by better managing your time.
- You dedicate yourself to the important matters first—there is enough time for the urgent ones later.
- You give constant attention to all the major areas of your life.
- You are completely dedicated to the tasks that you have chosen and exercise integrity in the present moment.

Checklist
Create a list with all tasks facing you at the moment. Group these tasks in four categories:
1. important and urgent;
2. important and not urgent;
3. urgent and not important; and
4. not urgent and not important.

Remove all tasks from the third and fourth category from your to-do list. Gain space regularly for activities from Category 2. Begin to work in block hours. Start with your weekly scheduling. Integrate an hour of reflection into your weekly scheduling.

CHAPTER 10
BE ABUNDANT

INVITING OTHERS TO YOUR HORIZON

IT IS MAINLY UP TO US, TO CREATE A NATURAL AND ENJOYABLE RELATION-SHIP WITH OTHER PEO-PLE. I CANNOT STRESS THE IMPORTANCE OF GOOD HU-MAN RELATIONS ENOUGH, BECAUSE THERE IS NO REAL TRUE **HAPPINESS** WHEN THEY ARE IGNORED.

NORMAN VINCENT PEALE

ALTHOUGH IT IS NOW NORMAL TO BE CON-NECTED IN SOCIAL NET-WORKS, we still tend to define our worth in comparison and in competition with other people.

Many people believe that when one person gains, another person loses. The daily media are constantly classifying people in terms of **winners and losers.** This norm results in a tremendous **loss of reality and waste of manpower** that is not put into finding solutions—whether in language, thought or deed. What remains is the conviction:

I must be among the winners, because there are either winners or losers.

WE TEND TO THINK: If I can't be among the winners, then there is no other place for me than that of the losers. This way of thinking can turn children into bitter rivals or resigned victims. All too often the more sensitive people are predisposed to giving up. **As a result**, resignations are formed that can only later be corrected **with great difficulty and much effort**.

Individuality and diversity are banned and in their place are the same conventional models and get-ahead strategies in which weaknesses are compared with strengths, winners with losers. The result of all of this is that we are left with a general comparison ending in an average and mediocre goal.

The aim of your personal strategy must be to develop your individual strengths and to build a unique performance profile that will enable you to find the *lock* (job, project, work, customer) that fits your own individual *key* (unique personality and profile).

> *"Every man is a genius; however, if you judge a fish by his ability to climb trees, he will spend his whole life thinking he is stupid."*
> ~ (attributed to) Albert Einstein

Fish should be recognized in their own medium as being as successful as the monkey, but if the ability to climb trees is considered to be more worthwhile, the monkey wins over the fish, as all the unique qualities that the underwater world has to offer are devalued.

In modern culture, we place less of an emphasis and value on such traits as collegiality, interdependence, teamwork, tolerance, acceptance, and joy in the success of others. This way of thinking does not suggest we are taking a lofty attitude about such traits; rather it shows we have a fear of losing and a sense of scarcity.

We are of the conviction that *there is enough for everyone* in the world and that peace can only prevail when all have received their fair share.

The chart below highlights the contrast between two life-shaping attitudes—the attitude of deficit and the attitude of abundance. These attitudes impact our speech, thoughts and actions.

Characteristics, attitude, mentality	Deficit	Abundance
Speech	◊ Reactive ◊ Emphasis on limitations ◊ Emphasis on recurring injustices and the past ◊ Judging people who live in abundance	◊ Open ◊ Constitutive ◊ Emphasis on opportunities ◊ Emphasis on the present and future ◊ Powerful and with support opposition from others
Thoughts	◊ May I have this? ◊ That is unfair. ◊ Why don't I have more? ◊ Now it's my turn!	◊ I am worth it! ◊ It is possible step by step. ◊ How can I give value? ◊ How can I accomplish the next step?
Feelings	◊ Disadvantaged ◊ Jealous ◊ Angry ◊ Disappointed ◊ Sober	◊ Blessed ◊ Gifted ◊ Joy over others' success ◊ Elated ◊ Responsible
Actions	◊ Characterized by hedging one's own position ◊ Restricted, closed ◊ Restrained ◊ Risk-averse	◊ Influenced by the establishment of mutual value ◊ Creative, constructive, open ◊ Sharing ◊ Risk taker
Attitude	◊ There is not enough for both of us; therefore I'll take my part first. ◊ So far I have fallen short, now it's my turn. ◊ I need to hurry and get my part before it is too late.	◊ There is enough for us both; how can we each benefit? ◊ We will work together to accomplish the assignment and share the results fairly. ◊ We will view things on a long-term basis and cooperate to achieve our results.

What kind of speaking, thinking, feeling, action, or attitude prevails in you? Are you a person of abundance, joyfully giving and accepting without conditions, or do you tend to hold on to things, penny pinching and being as independent as possible in order to not be in debt to others? Examine yourself honestly: To which category do you belong; do you belong to the category with which you want to be associated? Invite others to join you on your way to your new horizon.

Title	Description of attitude	Features
Lose-Lose	◊ Shaped by a fearful response ◊ Full of envy and criticism ◊ Little courage ◊ Little concern for others	◊ Disturbed and aggressive communication ◊ Both parties lose; there are no real winners ◊ Convinced that there can be only one solution: My way or no agreement – which is also a win-lose – this usually leads to lose-lose ◊ Rigid and without commitment ◊ Creates dependencies that are not healthy ◊ Is the long-term outcome of all interactions that are not based on win-win
Win-Lose	◊ Characterized by competition, comparison, power and powerlessness ◊ Authoritarian figure ◊ Power is the foundation ◊ Self-centered, ego-centric	◊ Use of power and position to come to a conclusion ◊ Lacking empathy for the other person's position ◊ Belief that there can only be one winner and that the advantage of the opponent means a disadvantage or sacrifice for the self ◊ Success is achieved at the expense of others
Win-Win	◊ Both parties win ◊ It's ok if it takes time to find a good solution ◊ Needs of both sides are integrated ◊ Total conviction of many alternative solutions ◊ Wants to win while allowing and wanting opponents to win, too	◊ Actively searching for mutual benefit ◊ Communication filled with active listening ◊ Intensive communication ◊ Creative ◊ Dedicated ◊ Respectful and cooperative

Three possible constellations for inviting others to join you are: Lose-Lose, Win-Lose and Win-Win.

The win-win attitude will improve the quality of your relationships. In return, sympathy, respect, trust and love will be shown to you. When maintained over time, a win-win attitude will mature into a win-win character.

People who have this win-win attitude never lose—they win in all aspects of their lives. You, too, can belong to this group of winners! Why should others object something that will aid your success when you are also helping them to succeed? People around you want you to progress when they sense that you want to bring everyone with you!

In business and political negotiations, deals and agreements, it is not always possible to make both parties equal winners. If a win-win situation can't be established at the time, *no* agreement should be made. Perhaps the time is not ripe or the conditions are too difficult. Or there is insufficient desire or energy to search for possible alternatives.

In the face of a non-agreement, the key points of each party should be examined bit by bit. If you are willing to accept one thing that the other party needs, and if the other person can do the same—even without full agreement, each side has a feeling of mutual appreciation. This forms a basis upon which to work.

By making it okay to say *No*, you can maintain mutual respect, and at a later time revisit the deal to see if a win-win solution is possible. You are then less likely to slide into a cheap compromise or flee into a win-lose or lose-lose agreement. You will choose not to make an agreement that does not create a win-win situation, because the relationship is too important to you. If you simply *agree to disagree* with feelings of friendship, appreciation and warmth, you can still connect, even where no connection previously seemed possible.

What is a true *win-win* in the business world? *Could it be defined as an* entrepreneur-stakeholder deal? Perhaps it's the type of deal in which employees are allowed to participate in the true entrepreneurial success of the company, while the company achieves even higher sales at the same time.

Win-win can be so easy: You pay five dollars for five delicious pretzels at a bakery you trust. You satisfy your appetite and the baker makes money for his livelihood.

Many companies are now led with win-lose strategies. One prominent example can be found in the Samwer brothers, who founded Rocket Internet. They are known to mimic successful e-commerce companies in Silicon Valley and to resell them.[50] Oliver Samwer was quoted as saying: "In the end we are entrepreneurs that say 'Whatever it takes.'"[51] So the first deal the Samwer brothers made was a clone of the internet auction house eBay, which was sold to the eBay founders four months later. This approach to business is characterized by disrespect and indecency. It's a perfect example of win-lose as the Samwer brothers enrich themselves at the expense of others.

Truly remarkable win-win stories in business usually take place over a long period of time. One of them, the German company *Vorwerk*, has operated for more than 130 years. Currently it is breaking company records with a total return of 2.8 billion euros in 2014, making it the third largest group in direct sales worldwide.[52] The two most famous products in Germany—the vacuum cleaner Kobold and the kitchen multifunction machine Thermomix—constitute the two main pillars of the company with two-thirds of total sales. The

---

50 Cf. Dörner S., Fuest B., Seibel K., *Das rätselhafte Firmengeflecht Rocket Internet*, 05/27/2015, in www.welt.de, http://www.welt.de/wirtschaft/webwelt/article141524662/Das-raetselhafte-Firmengeflecht-Rocket-Internet.html, accessed on 09/09/2015

51 Cf. Mac R., *Germany's Samwer Brothers to become billionaires with Rocket Internet IPO*, 07/31/2014, in www.forbes.com, http://www.forbes.com/sites/ryanmac/2014/07/31/samwer-brothers-billionaires-rocket-internet-ipo/2/, accessed on 09/09/2015

52 Cf. Koch B., *Thermomix-Boom beflügelt Vorwerk*, in Frankfurter Allgemeine Zeitung, 05/21/2015, http://www.faz.net/aktuell/wirtschaft/thermomix-boom-teurer-kuechengeraete-befluegelt-staubsauger-hersteller-vorwerk-13605125.html, accessed on 09/09/2015, cf. www.vorwerk.de, Familienunternehmen mit Tradition, http://corporate.vorwerk.de/de/portraet/, accessed on 09/09/2015

company's core business is direct selling[53] (selling from person to person without intermediaries or a sales counter). In this business model, representatives usually receive no fixed salary but participate directly in the success of the company through commissions for their own contributions. The win-win in this business model is the symbiosis of business and partner sales growth. Without the other, both cannot survive, but with each other both can experience exponential gains.

TIP

SEE
Your attitude and approach. Ask yourself: Are you comfortable inviting others to join you in the pursuit of your horizon? Are your invitations win-win?

DO
A. Think of one professional experience and one personal experience that illustrate a win-lose situation. Now find a common approach to resolve this situation. Identify so-called *losing thoughts*, the negative attitudes and reactions to the situation for each example identified. In addition, identify *win-win thoughts*, positive attitudes and proactive interpretations for each example.

---

53   Cf. www.vorwerk.de, Familienunternehmen mit Tradition, http://corporate. vorwerk.de/de/portraet/, accessed on 09/09/2015

Professional experience

Losing thoughts	Win-win thoughts

Personal experience

Losing thoughts	Win-win thoughts

Win-Win Agreement Scheme
- *Task clarification:* At the start of a project, clarify the type of cooperation, intended goals and desired results.

- *Stakeholders*: At the beginning, discuss which people or organizations are part of the agreement and which are not.
- *Rules of communication*: Clearly determine the rules of communication. In what form (emails, letters, phone calls, meetings, appointments) and with what frequency will the communication take place? Define the coordination and communication routine, and set the limits and expectations in the defined area. Determine deadlines for the agreement.
- *Resources:* What resources are available or easily accessible for you? What are the financial, technical, organizational, structural or human resources?[54]
- *Responsibility*: Which individual person is responsible for which result or responsibility? The term "individual" is consciously chosen. When members of a team have true responsibility for each other, the team becomes an "us." A team does not have the same responsibility as an individual. The reference to a natural individual creates accountability, awareness and results. How will success be measured? How will progress be reported to all those involved? How often will this occur?
- *Consequences*: What are the (mutually agreed upon) negative consequences for deviations and violations? What are the positive rewards for effort and earnings? What are the positive and negative consequences for other contingencies?

B. Abundance Mentality

Lose-lose and win-lose interactions and relationships arise from a mentality of "too little." One believes: "There is not enough for everyone, so I want to have my share first."

You cultivate a mindset of abundance by being convinced that there is a mutually acceptable alternative that provides enough for both sides. You cultivate the abundance mentality by actively seeking alternatives and searching for the win for

---

54 In the context of work, human resources can be: employees, team resources, etc. In the private context: self, family members, friends, etc.

both sides with intent. For this you need to remain flexible and continually accept that your view may be one-sided. Asking for external help and wise counsel can be helpful here and worth the extra effort.

C. Negotiating conditions for win-win

Effective deals are based on the attitude that both parties are equally served. They assume a mutual understanding of the current situation and desired future. Try using the abundance attitude and draw up a personal and professional win-win agreement as practice.

Justin: Early in my career I was fortunate to work with Stephen R. Covey. We did an impressive project with *Shea Homes*, a division of the billion-dollar JF Shea Company. Paul Kalkbrenner, VP of Construction at Shea Homes, transformed the home building industry in Arizona using the concept of win-win agreements.

I first met Paul when he invited me to visit a building site at 4:45 am. A.M.!? I had never been to a client appointment at 4:45 a.m. in the morning.

At the job site I watched Paul review a win-win agreement with his site superintendent and the owners from different trades, also known as sub-contractors. I learned that Paul was using the concept of win-win agreements to solve serious conflicts that were negatively impacting Shea Homes.

At that time, Shea Homes was the 3rd largest residential home builder in Arizona. Due to a tight labor market with intense competition, relationships between trades had deteriorated from a friendly network of tradesman to a confrontational, cut-throat environment. The plumber, for example, no longer took time to socialize with the framer. In fact, there was a good chance the framer was upset with the plumber for messing up his framing, which required extra trips back to the house and expensive rework. The fun of seeing fellow tradesmen on the work site was slipping away. Shea Homes' leaders were spending a significant amount of their time as referees between trades.

I was even more surprised later that afternoon when Paul had me help him carry a cooler full of cold drinks into a partially finished home. Inside the front room sat a dozen workers around a flipchart. The owner of Shea Homes, a plumbing company, was teaching a group of workers from multiple trades Stephen Covey's 4th Habit: Think Win-Win. Watching workers sit on buckets in shorts, no shirts, tool belts on the ground, and a Seven Habits manual in their lap was something I had never even considered!

Later that night Paul explained his strategy. He had created win-win agreements with several of the best trades in the Phoenix area. He promised them preferred status with Shea in exchange for their commitment, as company owners, to become certified in teaching Covey's *Seven Habits* and help him teach those habits to the workers of all the other trades.

This group of trade owners then worked together to map out the end-to-end home building process. They created win-win agreements for how they would work together to improve relationships between workers and the performance of each other's companies.

Within five years, Shea Homes Arizona became the largest home builder in the state and the number one performing division of JF Shea. With a staff of 300 people, Shea Homes Arizona delivered 2,000 homes a year with $400 million passing through 33 trades!

GROW

The following affirmations and checklists will accelerate your growth.

Affirmations
- You believe that there is enough for me and you and everyone else.
- You have the desire and the power to look for alternatives that will satisfy all sides.
- Your long-term success is based only on mutual benefit.
- Your abundance mentality brings the right opportunities into your life.

Checklist
1. Integrate the mentality of abundance into your everyday life.
2. Implement the framework of *Build Relationships of Trust* (BROT) in conversations with family, friends, business partners and people with whom your relationship is strained.
3. Establish *win-win or no-deal* as the basic condition for all of your negotiations.
4. Don't break an arranged appointment—you are the owner of your trustworthiness.
5. Start to recognize win-lose and lose-lose situations and create a strategy to solve them.

CHAPTER 11
GO EXPONENTIAL

SEEKING SYNERGY

ALL OF US LIVE UNDER THE SAME SKY, BUT WE DON'T ALL HAVE THE SAME HORIZON.

KONRAD ADENAUER

TO LOVE PEOPLE IS THE ESSENCE OF MORALITY; TO KNOW PEOPLE THE ESSENCE OF WISDOM.

CONFUCIUS (551 BC–479 BC)

On January 12, 2007 a man in ordinary clothes stood at an exit of an underground station in Washington, D.C., and began to play the violin. For 45 minutes the passers-by could hear music from Johann Sebastian Bach, Franz Schubert and other classical composers. Since it was rush hour, thousands passed by on their way to work.

During the first three minutes, one old man noticed the music. He walked slower, listened for a minute and then went on his way. Later the violinist received his first tip—a one-dollar bill that was thrown at his feet from a woman who didn't even stop. Then, someone leaned against a pillar for five minutes, then looked at the clock and hurried to the trains. The first person who was eager to listen to the violinist was a three-year old boy. However, his mother was in a hurry and pulled him away as he looked back longingly at the violinist. Other children also stopped to listen, but after two minutes their impatient parents pulled them away.

During the 43 minutes that he played, 1,097 pedestrians walked past him. He received $32.17. And of the seven people who stopped to listen to him, only one person recognized him and put $20 in his violin case. She spoke of great admiration for his work.

The name of the violinist was Joshua David Bell,[55] and he was participating in an experiment on human behavior conducted by Gene Weingarten of the *Washington Post* and filmed with a hidden camera[56]. Gene Weingarten received the Pulitzer Prize for journalism in 2008 for this article and what it had to say about the perception of human behavior.

Two days before, Joshua Bell had played in a sold-out concert hall in Boston, where the cheapest ticket was not to be had for under $100. He played with the same Stradivari[57], estimated to be worth about $3.5 million, in Boston as well as in the subway. The pieces that he played are considered among the most difficult pieces for a violinist.

---

55   Joshua David Bell, 1967, a U.S. Violinist

56   Film link to this experiment: tinyurl.com/32a32w

57   Antonio Stradivari, born: 1644, died: 1737, an Italian violin maker

When asked what he learned from this experiment, Joshua Bell said: *"People are unable to recognize beauty outside of the context in which a work of art is usually admired."*

Educated Observation

The observations that we make are all too often compared to what other people around us perceive, and they then get adjusted, as the Bell experiment clearly shows. The difficulty is to stay an individual and yet comply with the prevailing standards and classifications of our society.

We are part of an incomprehensibly large and complex social system. We do not live alone and isolated in an abstract world of ideas, but are constantly interacting with thousands of things and people who regularly play a part in our lives.

We are provided with a continuous connection to the world around us through our senses of sight, hearing, smell, taste and touch. Throughout our lives we have the opportunity to meet many people. Our ability to make key observations depends on how well we integrate with others and how alert we are during these interactions. How good are you at observing others? How good is your knowledge of human nature and your ability to perceive others fairly? How alert are you in dealing with both people who know you and those who are new to you?

How can you train yourself to be more careful in your observations with others? Too often we run mindlessly through our lives without looking around us, without perceiving others and our environment, and without being aware of all that is going on. Our lives are enriched when we tap into our childhood ability to feel intensely, to be amazed at simple things, to delight in discovery and thereby understand the world around us more fully.

In order to perceive our environment and receive high-quality impressions, our different sensory organs must be cared for and supported. We need to protect our senses from abuse (e.g., from loud music, laser light, excessive television, etc.) and strengthen them through regular use.

*The fashion industry thrives on observation and perception.
Through fashion we show who we are. Fashion reflects social
codes. Through it, we show what kind of person we are—from
the homeless to the CEO. Every social and economic class has its
own "uniform." Thanks to the designers of our world, we can
turn our insides out. Every season, millions of people redesign
themselves. They wear (or copy) the looks of the catwalks of the
world, when the latest fashion shows in Milan, Paris and New
York take place.*

*One man who has influenced the fashion of our time like no
other is **Karl Lagerfeld**. Vogue magazine calls him "the
German designer, who succeeds in everything. He led large
couture houses such as Chanel, Chloé or Fendi for years to
immense success and casually designs for his own fashion
lines."[58]*

*Karl Lagerfeld followed the principle of observation and
perception holistically. He designed every detail of his creations,
from the draft to the finished model. Yet his overall view
includes significantly more than designing a garment. He also
develops the theme of the collection, does his own research, and
pays attention to the details and authenticity. Even the styling
of the fashion show and product marketing are supervised by
him. Yet whilst under great time pressure, he designed the
invitation cards for Chanel's fashion show.[59]*

Fashion and its famous German designer Karl Lagerfeld
reflect living with intent and its principles at the core. Fashion
shows the enormous importance of even the smallest details,
which we can perceive in ourselves and other people, and thus
the fundamental content of the principle of observation and
perception.

---

58 Cf. www.vogue.de, http://www.vogue.de/tags/l/karl-lagerfeld, accessed on
08/28/2015

59 Cf. www.horstson.de, http://horstson.de/modemethode-karl-lagerfelds-
kosmos-in-bonn/2015/03/, accessed on 08/31/2015

With regular practice, you can train your senses to perceive impressions faster, more perfectly and more precisely in order to implement them in your personal life and business.

An impulse received from one of our senses can be completed by the other. They are the *basis* for any insight and judgment we receive and thus become the basis for everything we think, feel and do. The more accurate our impressions, the more consequential our decisions.

Of course we are responsible for the next step of evaluating the impulses we receive, which is also a learning process. However, in all cases, if the initial conclusion is wrong then the resulting outcomes will be flawed. Your impressions help you to form opinions as to why things happen, which are then processed by your intellect, after which you should then seek to discover the *deeper meaning*.

What Is Important Now

Before you start evaluating your impressions, you first need to train your powers of observation and perception through conscious use. Learn to observe *without* evaluating at the same time. The ability to observe without evaluating will open the doors of *synergy* in your life.

"The whole is greater than the sum of the individual parts."
~ Aristotel

"Strength lies in differences, not in similarities."
~ Stephen R. Covey

This principle of being collectively bigger, stronger and more effective than the total of the individual efforts applies equally in any organization, including families. Remember: ***Combined unity is much stronger than the sum of its individual parts.***

In a campfire, the embers in the middle of the fire are the strongest. If you move a piece of burning, glowing wood one meter away from the fire you will see that in just a matter of seconds, the flame will flicker as the wood gets colder. Put the wood back in the middle of the glowing fire and within seconds it will begin to catch fire and glow again.

We are still a long way away from learning all there is to know about the importance and meaning of vibrancy produced by proximity and being connected. We know little compared to all there is to know about the importance and significance in the response that comes from closeness and affiliation. We only see the sobering results as families break up due to insufficient interchange and lack of common ground. Relationships remain distant rather than become more meaningful and rewarding.

We see both positive and negative synergy in relationships and teams. When positive synergy occurs in the leadership of teams and global organizations, we see the results in live exchanges, confidence, resonance, trust and power. When negative synergy occurs, we see the results in lost opportunities and distrust. If negative synergy is not converted into positive synergy, it inevitably leads to greater distance or separation. A pervasive air of negative synergy can create hostile, even life-threatening conditions and environments for people.

We might imagine these synergies as spirals, either a continual upward path or a continual downward path.

Think about logs. Through the cooling process, there is no more interchange and no mutual support or conception. The relationship is empty and each party withdraws into itself. For the burning log, it is the absence of the warmth and embers of other logs that causes it to cool faster than normal.

Positive synergy inevitably leads to new results and common horizons. Aristotle, a student of Plato and teacher of Alexander the Great, composed this famous sentence—"The whole is more than the sum of its parts." Two-way dependence (interdependence), networking, mutual enrichment and the nurturing of one another bring forth new and valuable experiences and ideas. This interdependence can repeatedly be seen in our professional and personal lives and can be a daily experience.

German car companies are perfect examples for the skillful use of synergies. Through joint projects both within and outside their own sector, these companies are developing the future of automobiles in the world. Mercedes-Benz presented the F 015, a self-driving concept car, at the exhibition Consumer Electric Show (CES) 2015 in Las Vegas. [60] The "eyes" of this car are stereo cameras, which support autonomous braking, Lane Keeping Assist and Traffic Sign Recognition. The stereo cameras are supplied by the South Korean electronics manufacturer LG. [61] In this case these two companies see themselves as sparring partners and develop pioneering products by always concentrating on their own core strike zones, automobile manufacturing and electronics, and therefore achieving top results and trendsetting innovations in their areas of specialization.

Most people are social beings who naturally desire synergy; however, seeking and achieving positive synergy is a life-long process. Achieving and sustaining synergy requires that we perceive and respond to each other. How can we make ourselves more open and more sensitive to the many verbal and non-verbal signals of those around us? Synergy creates personal and professional success. It enables us to be connected with other people. We can't find a truly successful and effective person who does not use the art and power of synergy.

Think about what you want most in life. Can you achieve or obtain it without interacting with others? Most likely not. Most unsuccessful and unhappy people have given up on creating synergy with other people. Sometimes we hear people boasting that *they don't need anyone.* This is not the point—it is not about whether we "need" someone, because we can't make

---

60 Cf. www.autobild.de, *Neue Details zum Zukunfts-Benz,* http://www.autobild.de/artikel/mercedes-f-015-vorstellung-5429797.html, accessed on 08/27/2015

61 Cf. www.autobild.de, *Neue Augen für Mercedes,* 12/30/2014, http://www.autobild.de/artikel/ces-2015-daimler-kooperiert-mit-lg-5517649.html, accessed on 10/27/2015

"it" on our own, rather it's about working together with positive synergy to produce exponential results.

Synergy is defined as the joint creation of results and conditions by two or more people who then create something that each individual on their own could not have achieved. Let's contrast "true synergy" with counterfeit or negative synergy.

	True synergy	Counterfeit synergy
Speech	Results oriented	Problem oriented
Thoughts	Emphasis on possibility	Emphasis on giving up / losing
Action	Characterized by cooperation, mutual decisions	Characterized by competition – promoting yourself only
Attitude	Process oriented, open to results	Single-sided solution oriented, structured obsessive

We people need each other in order to get ahead in life. The entrepreneur needs his employees to relieve him of some of his work. The employees need the entrepreneur, who in turn pays them their earned salary. The self-employed businessman needs customers who buy his goods. A writer needs a publisher who agrees to publish and market his works. Success in life depends on the cooperation and good will of those around us. We need to know how to treat people for enabling us to reach our objectives. In order to do this, we need to put ourselves in the position of those with whom we want to cooperate.

Synergetic relationships are the results of three behavior patterns: 1) the perceptions of those around us; 2) the putting aside of prejudices and judging of others; and 3) empathy.

Get to know the people in your immediate vicinity better. Talk to them; learn about their likes and dislikes, needs and interests; ask questions that require more than a "yes" or "no" answer; and listen without personal bias. Try to understand how the person has arrived where he is today. Make your observations with a kind disposition. Often what we observe does not prevent us from achieving synergy—our own convictions get in the way. Biased convictions hinder us from seeing the originality and worth of those around us and prevent us from opening up, speaking to others as equals, and celebrating the differences. As we treat others with respect, we see their abilities, talents, experience and strength.

> *What is, is allowed to be.*
> *What is allowed to be,*
> *can express itself.*
>
> *What can express itself*
> *in the appropriate way…*
> *…creates change,*
> *…and finds peace.*
>
> ~ *Elke Hatzelmann, Augsburg*

Equal Right to Be Understood

If we adapt the attitude that an interaction will bring better results and that we want to understand the views and beliefs of those around us, we assume that they *really* have the same rights as we do. This is a platform of equality that creates a productive and blossoming common ground.

A person who has this inner attitude can relax. He can become creative, as he no longer is engaged in the power struggle of always needing to be right. On the contrary, he can do everything; he can for example use his *and* the other person's input to create great financial wealth or other indications of success. He doesn't have to exclude anything in order to prove that his ideas were the best. Thus, equality and a great abundance of resources give us the best foundation for change—as well as the achievement of synthesis and synergy.

Here are Stephen Covey's five ascending steps for celebrating the differences and creating synergy: 1) tolerance; 2) acceptance; 3) recognition; 4) appreciation; and 5) celebration.

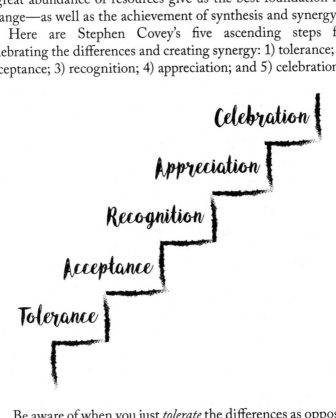

Be aware of when you just *tolerate* the differences as opposed to when you start to *accept* the other's opinions. Continuing down the steps, be aware when you are more than just *accepting* the person's opinions, and are now *recognizing* a different point of view; be aware again when you *appreciate* another's input, and when you *celebrate* the differences as an individual, family, team, or organization.

Striving daily to develop more synergy in your life will enable you to express yourself in a way to others that will enable a mutual appreciation. It is the golden key of diplomacy.

Below we show you some exercises for creating synergy. We encourage you to try completing the exercises that you find interesting and adapt them to your personal situation.

TIP

SEE—You need to know well the people with whom you deal, whether it's your boss, employees or colleagues. Observe carefully everyone you meet—their appearance and countenance can give you valuable insights into their character. Skillful observation opens the doors to synergy with people around you.

Reflection: Is negative synergy evident in some of your personal relationships? Which ones? In which relationships is harmony repeatedly disrupted due to personal differences not being accepted? What do you think you would lose by cultivating an inner attitude of appreciation? Do you feel unappreciated and thus need to prove who is stronger or right in order to feel validated? Do you have idealistic requirements or inflated expectations of others?

DO—Exercises in Observation

A. Take a walk. On most streets, the right side is different from the left. On one side, we might encounter people who casually stroll past the luxury and fashion shops; on the other side we may see busy people hurrying about their business among large bank buildings.

As you walk through the streets of your hometown, try to see the differences between one side of the street and the other and try to explain the difference.

If you live in the countryside, stop to observe the scenery. Try to fathom the relationship between the type of plants, soil condition and location of the field or garden. Observe the behavior of the animals during different seasons or changes in weather.

B. In-depth observation and association

Open an atlas and carefully consider the map of a country whose history and culture is well known to you, or one to which you like to go on holiday. Then close the atlas and try to draw the map from memory—not with all the details but in broad terms, taking the size ratios into consideration. Ask yourself how the shapes of this country and its location in the world have influenced its fate.

C. Observation without prejudice and evaluation

Take a familiar object, such as a stone, in your hand. Start to describe what you see. For example: I see a solid thing, almost egg-shaped, smooth, grayish with white lines, notched on one side, about 14 inches wide. The description should *not* include: "This is a stone that looks like ...". *Stone* is the classification of what we think we see. The details are not questionable, but the name *stone* is. Is it a stone or papier-mâché? We only know when we touch it, but from an observation point of view it is actually just a theory.

D. Train your perception

The following exercise will help you train your perception of those around you. We encourage you to do this exercise regularly and continuously. Proceed as follows:

1. Memorize the name (correct spelling) of a person you want to observe.
2. Guess his or her age.
3. Compare his size and stature with yours and with other people whom you know. According to Goethe, everything visible is only a simile. We might also say: "Similar forms, similar content."
4. Consider exactly the head, hair, forehead, eyes, nose, mouth, chin, cheeks, ears, skin and facial expressions of the person. Describe your first impression in one word.
5. Look at the person's hands. Are they big or small? Do they appear delicate, rough, clumsy, nervous or sensitive?
6. Are the person's clothes chosen with care and style? Are they sporty, modern and old-fashioned? Appraise and pay attention to the cleanliness and condition of his clothing.

7. Observe how he moves and walks; listen for a moment to the sound of his footsteps and think about whether you would be able to recognize him from his walk.

8. Pay attention to voice, speech and possible accent. Subtle mistakes in pronunciation and barely audible voice fluctuations can reveal many secrets.

9. Look closely at the eyes—the movement, what they tell you and how clear they are. The eyes are the "windows to the soul" and speak their own language. What do you see in the eyes? What you feel when they look at you?

10. Describe in a few words, what feelings this person triggers in you. Write the results of your perceptions and impressions in your learning diary.

Under no circumstances, judge another person as having few or less valuable abilities; instead, see him or her as a whole person. Be open and observant to all that is shown to you. The result of observing someone once should not be a final judgment; rather the final judgment should be a collection of impressions that triggers various feelings that will speak to you.

Be open to seeing them differently the second or third time. Everyone has good and bad days—just as you do.

Exercises for Creating Synergy

A. Synergistic Mindset

The first step to profitable change is to be consciously aware of the situation and to admit what you recognize. Seeing the present situation in all its dimensions does not necessarily mean that you agree with it, or that the situation remains permanent—it is only necessary in order to facilitate change.

The second step is to refrain from asking yourself what would happen if you gave up the idea of personal recognition—of always having to be right, needing to be the best, or having others live up to your ideal expectations. Give others the same rights as you enjoy. How? Think of a person with whom you have some disagreements. Decide not to react but to observe yourself when the person does things that you don't like. What is so bad about what they are doing?

You can acknowledge and accept the differences in people. You can admit that those differences have enriched your life. You can not only live and let live but also praise and even celebrate the differences of others!

What will you do today, this week, and each month in order to create a positive synergy in your personal and professional relationships?

Again, think about a person with whom you have negative synergy. See yourself allowing the other person to prevail, overlooking the alleged wrongs and accepting the other person for whom he or she is. What happens in your imagination when you do this?

Who or what can help you to enhance the synergy in these relationships? You might think of a family member, mediator, friend or a neutral space for meetings.

B. Mental preparation: Money

Suppose that you need a large sum of money in order to carry out a planned project. Ask yourself who (a person you trust) could loan you the money. How would you go about getting the loan? What advantages would the investor have, if he or she loaned you the money? Why have you chosen this person to borrow money from? How do you deal with the repayment?

C. Finding the right time: Timing

Success depends 99% on timing. Imagine that you are a musician in an orchestra. Each instrument has its own sound and plays an important part in making each piece of music sound special. The conductor usually sets the tempo, but you manage your own timing, the notes and rhythm. From the musical score you can find the tact and tempo for your piece in order for you to be fully integrated into the whole orchestral movement. If you play the notes at the wrong time, the whole piece of music sounds "off."

The same applies to the timing of your success. Always look for the most favorable time for a conversation. If you hear a "no" in the evening—you might hear a "yes" in the morning.

Timing has two dimensions—taking action and being patient. You need to find the right balance. Time sometimes works for you, but it can also work against you. Do not give people the chance to dismiss your concerns and requests purely because you have chosen an inopportune time to discuss them. With whom or on what matters could you improve your timing? How?

GROW—The following affirmations and checklist will accelerate your growth:

Affirmations
- You believe that together we are stronger.
- You see people being different from you as potential for enrichment.
- You are all in the same boat.
- One plus one can equal more than two!

Checklist
1. Broaden your mind by developing the ability to judge people, things and situations on a meta-level without any prejudices.
2. Learn to pay attention to small things.
3. Study your conversation partners. Learn to draw conclusions from your observations.
4. Learn to make observations independently on the situation.
5. Mind your surroundings and be curious, even in your daily commute to work.
6. Mind occasional conventions and social rules.
7. Learn to listen correctly.
8. Learn to profit and grow from accepting different points of view.
9. Put yourself in your counterparts' shoes to learn through empathy about their motives.

10.Learn to value, accept and celebrate differences.
11.Reject status symbols as the criteria for finding or fostering relationships.
12. Seek the right timing for important decisions with business partners.

CHAPTER 12
PREPARE
FOR CRISIS

WALKING
BEYOND THE
RUNWAY

I CALL THAT MAN AWAKE WHO, WITH **CONSCIOUS KNOWLEDGE** AND **UNDERSTANDING**, CAN PERCEIVE THE DEEP UNREASONING **POWERS** IN HIS SOUL, HIS WHOLE INNERMOST **STRENGTH**, **DESIRE** AND **WEAKNESS**, AND KNOWS HOW TO RECKON WITH HIMSELF.

HERMAN HESSE, NARCISSUS AND GOLDMUND

Thomas: During my life's journey, I have been privileged to meet some very special people. One of them is my friend and flight instructor Norbert S., whom I met for the first time in the early 1980's on a gliding field in Bavaria, South Germany. About 10 years later he prepared me for a flight across the English Channel in a single-engine old-timer airplane built in 1940.

My pilot's license had expired, and I simply wanted to renew it; however, I received much more as Norbert trained very hard with me! I received a training that would save my life.

At that time I had a different opinion; in fact, part of me was annoyed with Norbert. But he was looking into the future and foreseeing a problem. As a manager and entrepreneur, I am accustomed to testing the limits of what is possible. In flying, however, this notion can be fatal! Norbert taught me to alter my normal perceptions and habits to learn vigilance and proactive problem solving. For example, dozens of times he had me turn the engine off in beautiful weather and during the most wonderful flights. On every flight he simulated some emergency. I slowly began to be aware of precisely what was happening to me: I was becoming more confident in my flying. Through his training, I was becoming prepared for all possible emergencies.

Norbert said: *"Any emergency that you are neither mentally nor physically prepared for has the capacity to throw you completely off balance. The emergencies that you have mentally and physically prepared for are less threatening and make you less afraid. Forward thinking replaces hectic and panic in challenging situations."*

In spite of my protestations that I didn't need to be so prepared, he persisted, saying I needed to know more in order to pass his flying requirements. He predicted that I would experience a crisis in this and in other aircraft. However, I was very relaxed. I had already mastered most of the potential difficult situations, learning how to handle: a burning oil tank; a forced landing at night; a total vision loss in an old airplane in a snowstorm; ice on both wings over Dresden without a deicer; and engine failure during a test flight. But he retained his position that I needed more preparation and was not impressed by my exceptional experience. He insisted on this point: *"You are either prepared and will survive to tell the story, or you will be among those who do not survive and have nothing left to tell."*

Several years and many flight hours later, I was making a flight in my old red Klemm 35. It was a beautiful late summer day. I had just completed a flight with my oldest son. Since I had a guest from London at the airport, I had planned a routine flight around the airfield with a flyover, so that the guest could photograph the plane from the ground.

I taxied alone to the runway for take-off. I was very familiar with the aircraft; in fact, I completed my first flight at age nine in this German aircraft—a Klemm 35 D, built in 1938. Now at age 39 I went with a lot of experience to the takeoff-run in the direction 09, exactly to the East.

I knew almost every nut and bolt on this aircraft. The cockpit was as familiar to me as my own coat pocket. Before beginning, I went back through the checklist and repeated all my routines for take-off and emergency landing—as Norbert had drilled into me—even though all the other pilots had told me that it was not necessary to do this in an old-timer airplane.

The flight began like any other that I had done before, but ended up in a completely different way. I was ready. As I gave full throttle, the plane moved along the 3,000-feet runway. I took off and the plane climbed, flying with the evening sun shining on my shoulder.

Then, seconds later, 150 feet in front of an electricity pylon, the engine stopped—it just completely cut out! It didn't even stutter—it just stopped dead. The blue sunlit sky changed within a second to pitch black dark without a trace of moonlight. Everything was completely hazy. Stunned, I stared into an old airspeed indicator.

The silence was eerie and reinforced the feeling of being completely alone and abandoned. But at the same time I felt a spark of gratitude that my young son Kai was not with me, as he had been in the flight just minutes before.

Thinking through everything that I had learned up to that moment, I knew that while making the more common choice of using an inversion curve[62] to return to land was tempting, it would most likely lead to death. I also knew that I did not want to rush straight into that farm and the electricity pylon.

I knew that the moment of truth had arrived. Would my skills, training and luck make it possible for me to survive? I only had about five seconds—that's 300 milliseconds! The clock was ticking. I was losing altitude. I could not negotiate or equivocate—at an altitude of only 450 feet, and the first 100 feet were already gone!

I wished that I wasn't alone or that I could make contact with the control tower—the silence, the solitude was so scary. But those were not options. Time was running out; the ground was coming closer.

When I look back on the situation, I know that I had switched over to my "inner autopilot." All the hours, days, weeks, and years of training in simulated emergencies with Norbert were now present and available to me. In that moment, I imagined that I heard him say: "First fly the aircraft." I did not care that another machine had started behind me; it did not matter now what the Tower was saying to me—all I could perceive was the altimeter and airspeed indicator and sense that the ground was coming closer and closer, although everything seemed to be frozen in slow motion.

That afternoon, I learned that there are moments in life when all that matters is *you* and what you can call up from the reserves of *your* inner self. In the next 5 milliseconds I lived

---

62 The *inversion curve* is the manoeuvre that a pilot usually unthinkingly, regardless of height, speed, load and wind conditions initiates after an engine failure just after take-off. It is the obsessive desire to want to return to the safety of the runway.

with more purpose and more focus than in any of the billions of milliseconds before.

Against all textbook opinions I decided to make an inversion curve. I focused and used all my mental force to push the stick forward, which seemed urgently necessary to avoid a crash.

To my surprise, however, my body and my muscles pulled the stick back! This is a natural reflex to want to steer the aircraft to go upwards (although neither the flight situation nor the speed of the aircraft do allow this) instead of steering forward and thereby down towards the ground, which is the *only* way to catch up speed again and not going into a spin due to lack of speed. The instinctive reaction to pull up is usually fatal; no speed will normally result in that the aircraft will be spinning within seconds towards the ground. As I crouched forward I mentally pressed the joystick forward and exercised all of my mental and psychological strength to mentally push against the pressures of my hands and arms wanting to and pulling back.

After an enormous internal battle, my mental strength won against the instinct of my muscles—and that saved my life.

An old flying joke states: "Any landing that you can walk from is a good landing." It was indeed a good landing because I survived it! But I couldn't actually walk for a while—my knees were still shaking for over an hour after I landed!

All my preparation had enabled me to make the right decisions when it mattered most. Thanks to Norbert, I had learned my lesson. If he had not been my flight instructor for so many years, I would not be writing these lines today!

I know now that the outcome of the flight was clear, long before that late summer day, long before I ever started the Hirth HM 504 engine, long before I even took off. The outcome—that I would survive—wasn't clear because I was an extremely talented pilot or because I was lucky—it was clear because I had listened and done my homework; however, it was also the last time that I flew that plane!

Even though the flight only lasted five minutes, those minutes changed my life forever, because I learned that I can be safe by preparing for the future. *When the impossible appeared, I was prepared. On that day it became crystal clear that I can overcome the crises of my life, as long as I'm prepared; all that needs to happen is that I imagine a possible outcome.*

Just like the motto says: "Expect the worst, hope for the best." We hope that you never find yourself in an existential crisis like the one I survived. But we do not know what situations life will bring you. However, the odds are that you will face crisis in your life. Prepare now and beat the odds!

> *"The price of freedom is constant vigilance."*
> ~ *Thomas Jefferson*

A basic principle of risk management is that by preparing and mentally anticipating potential crises and risks, you are most likely the master of the situation and the result. I hope and wish that this is the case for you in your personal and professional life.

In the professional area, we all experience crises and misfortunes. Some, unfortunately, never recover from those challenges. Most find, after a time, a way back to normalcy. Very few turn the adversity into a positive advantage.

*One such person is **Azim H. Premji**. When his father died in 1966, he experienced his first life-changing blow of fate. He dropped his engineering studies at Stanford University and returned to his native India, where he took over the family business, called Western Indian Vegetable Products. At this time, the company had a revenue of two million dollars with edible oils. He began to diversify into soap, wax and light bulbs. In 1977, India sealed off from the world economy, forcing Azim H. Premji to radically rebuild his company, transforming it into a computer hardware manufacturer* [63] *The second stroke of fate came along when India opened up for more competitive imports back into the 1990's. He was again forced to*

---

63   Cf. Dorfs, J., *Die Herausforderer. 25 neue Weltkonzerne, mit denen wir rechnen müssen*, Munich, 2007, p. 215

realign the company completely from the ground up and began to export IT services. [64]

Today, his company WIPRO employs more than 160,000 employees in over 175 cities on six continents with annual revenue of 7.6 billion dollars in 2015 [65], *for which Premji receives worldwide recognition. Business Week titled the former edible oil manufacturer in 2003 as "India's Tech King." Fortune listed him as one of the 25 most powerful economic leaders outside the US (2003) and Forbes called him one of the 10 most powerful people in the world in the field of "inducing change."* [66] *He's worth $16 billion, according to Forbes, is the third richest man in India and has received many high honors for his lifetime achievements and his contributions to society.* [67]

As painful as some of our experiences may be, Azim Premji shows us that even the most terrible tragedy—the loss of a parent— can be directed into a positive force moving forward. He inspires by not sticking his head in the sand, not lamenting and by not giving up. He inspires by showing strength amidst a crisis and by being prepared for future existence-threatening challenges.

Whenever I reconnect with the near plane crash experience that I shared earlier, I think of the title and subtitle of this chapter: "Prepare for Crisis: Walking beyond the runway" When I think of that incident, I think of my dear children, and of the pain and crises they will face in life. Then I ask myself: *Have I done enough to prepare them?* or *Have I been a good example of preparation and resilience?*

I deeply hope they remember, as my friend Ken Shelton wrote, that snakes are *everywhere* and that some may slither into our homes, into our very lives. We may think them

---

64 Cf. Dorfs, J., *Die Herausforderer. 25 neue Weltkonzerne, mit denen wir rechnen müssen,* Munich, 2007, p. 126ff.

65 Cf. www.wipro.com, http://www.wipro.com/about-wipro/, accessed on 08/31/2015

66 Cf. www.wipro.com, Azim H. Premji, http://www.wipro.com/about-Wipro/Wipro-leadership-team/Azim-H-Premji/, accessed on 08/31/2015

67 Cf. www.forbes.com, India's 100 Richest People. 2014 Ranking, http://www.forbes.com/india-billionaires/, accessed on 08/31/2015, cf. www.wipro.com, http://www.wipro.com/about-wipro/, accessed on 08/31/2015

harmless, but many are venomous (causing pain, addiction and disability), even lethal (causing death). We often presume that our pains are so personal that no one could possibly understand them, least of all a person who has never experienced the exact or similar pain. We may wonder how can people who advise and support us understand. How can the person living and being right next to me even grasp what I am going through?

Whatever specific conditions we face in the future, we can take the high road, the road less traveled. Our passion and compassion will go beyond sympathy and empathy and reach deep into the realm of our spiritual energy. Many times the pain that our loved ones are going through is so embedded in our souls that we experience it as if we are the ones living it. This is especially the case when our children face crisis and turmoil. If we are prepared and engaged we don't have to be a distant or casual observer of other people's life experiences. In every sense, we can then be a strong helping hand—full of grace and truth, mercy and merit.

The "venomous snakes" that seek to destroy us are *everywhere*—not just in some outback country canyons—and the best preventative antidote to snakebite is living with intent as part of fulfilling a meaningful mission in life. So, be prepared for the snakes that come your way—you will indeed be a resource and an inspiration to yourself and to others.

TIP

SEE—As Dr. Phil McGraw[68] notes, you will likely see *seven situations* that portend potential or probable crisis. These could be the worst seven days of your life. Prepare yourself for the probability that you will go through such days by doing the recommended activities in advance. You now have the power and clarity that would otherwise be missing in the situation, if and when you encounter it.

1. Loss—the day your heart breaks. We experience this first type of loss when we have to give up what we really value. Our identity is often personally interwoven with our relationships, jobs, careers and social recognition; when we experience loss in these areas, *it can shake us to the very foundations of our being.* Although this is an unpleasant thought, the reality is that such loss happens in life. In fact, the more we love certain people and appreciate certain things, the higher the probability of being injured through death, separation or change.

In order to prepare for this, ask yourself four questions:
- What are you doing to be in touch with your emotions? Have you found a creative way to examine and experience them? (Painting, crafts, drawing, music, etc.)
- Who among your closest family members and friends can you count on? What do these relationships need in order to continue to be strong now and at the time when you need their strength and support?
- Which group of people, team or personal relationships give you strength and energy that lets you refuel outside of your family?
- Do you celebrate your birthday, or even summer? We do not know how many more birthdays or summers we

---

68   Cf. www.forbes.com, India's 100 Richest People. 2014 Ranking, http://www.forbes.com/india-billionaires/, accessed on 08/31/2015, cf. www.wipro.com, http://www.wipro.com/about-wipro/, accessed on 08/31/2015 Dr. Phil McGraw, Real Life, Simon and Schuster, 2008

will see! Each season is infinitely valuable. What are you doing now and in the future to celebrate life with your loved ones?

2. Fear—the day you realize that you are driven by fear. You realize that fear is a strong force in your life and that it determines the way you live, why you live and what you do. You realize that perhaps with most major decision fear or the interests of others are taken more into account than your own inner compass? Ask yourself the following question and go deep in exploring: Does fear play a key role in your decisions?

In order to prepare, ask yourself these questions: What are you doing today either in your business or private life that is based on the fear of losing things—the fear of standing alone or with the minority? Where does the fear of loss affect your everyday life?

- What are you afraid of the most? What should not happen? What do you often think about that you want to avoid? The more you push something aside and try to prevent it, the more you give it the energy to grow and to push into your life. This is why it is important that you fully understand what your avoidance strategies are.
- Think about what could happen in your life if fear and worry gained even more influence over your sense of direction. If you were no longer clear about your life's direction, how would this impact your life?

3. Change—the day you realize that you are overwhelmed. Change requires adaptation, which is a dynamic process. This takes time, energy and strength. The day may come when you will need to make some changes and adjustments to your situation. The feeling of being overtaken and swallowed up by the demands of life, whether big or small, can begin to swamp you. Maybe you've noticed that you are no longer able to complete entire tasks. Perhaps you were once always the frontrunner, but now things have changed. Maybe your social connections are not as strong as you once thought they were. You now begin to ask yourself how you can get more money, strength, time, or contacts to bring you to the next step. This means that the process of change has caught up with you and you feel overwhelmed with the need to adjust to this new world of yours.

In order to prepare, ask yourself the following questions: How stable is your foundation? Upon what is your professional and financial framework built? Where have you built up collateral and fallback positions?

- If your position, your status, your influence or your reputation would change, what kind of ritual would you use to maintain or strengthen your inner happiness? Make a note to acknowledge where you find joy in life.
- To get into new waters, you must abandon the old view of the shore. This requires courage and determination. What three steps do you want to take or can you start to take today in order to begin on a new path?
- Many changes require complex answers and adjustments. At times, it may be too much for us. With the following so-called "salami tactics" or "salami-slice strategy," you can split up the toughest challenges. For example, only work on what is important for that day, and then take the next 24 hours and so forth. Or, you can use the salami tactics for the week, month or season. You sometimes feel stress and a sense of powerlessness when you set your focus too far ahead. Where can you implement the salami tactic today to help you on your path?

4. Health—the day in which the thing that you took for granted disappears. Another experience from my personal life: On a Sunday I danced in the garden with my beautiful two-year-old daughter, Sariah. It was a spring day and she seemed so full of life. The next day she suddenly had a high fever. With foreboding, my wife took her to the family doctor. Soon she called me, saying: "I'm on the way to Children's Hospital—Sariah has no white blood cells and will need to go into the intensive care unit." Our daughter had leukemia!

After going through years of chemotherapy, check-ups and various other medical procedures for my daughter, I now see clearly that the same thing could happen to me—tomorrow!

Occasionally we might spare a thought as to how it would be to receive such a telephone call. You, too, might one day be on the receiving end of such a call. The doctor is on the other end of the line, and he pauses for a moment before he speaks. You sense that his words will divide your life into a *before* and *after* the diagnosis. What follows is a storm crashing over you, impacting you first internally and then externally. He says: "The test results are positive," or "It's cancer," or "I have to notify you of a traffic accident..."

In the blink of an eye, you are in the middle of a different life than the one you thought you were living. You expect the worst and learn that it is even worse than you anticipated. Disease, trauma and accident never affect just one person, but all people in the environment. A trauma can impact the entire family—indeed, the whole society, and yet we seldom talk about it. Are you prepared? Do you have the necessary answers?

In order to prepare, ask yourself the following questions:

- Why is this happening to you? Why has your health, either in part or in its entirety, left you? What steps are you going to undertake?
- When the call comes, who is part of your "crisis team"? Who inside the family or who outside the family (friendly doctors, healers, counselors, etc.) is part of your team?
- Are you taking better care of your health these days? Which habits are your biggest problems? Have you set goals from the previous lesson that will enable you to lead a healthier lifestyle?
- No matter how bad the diagnosis—do you have a "bucket list"? The concept of a bucket list is an exercise in forward thinking. What you still want to experience or achieve before you "kick the bucket." Ask yourself what is important to you. You can have some really crazy ideas! You should definitely have one. What is on your bucket list? You may want to watch the film *The Bucket List* and start compiling a list today.

5. Mental Health—the day in which your self-possession leaves you. You want to go about your normal daily business on Monday, or you want to do something with family and friends on Friday. But then something happens that completely throws you off course. Perhaps it is the death of a friend or family member, the loss of your job, or a sudden dispute over an inheritance. You are deeply disappointed and feel that no one understands you anymore. Could it be that you do not comprehend all that is happening around you? Are you becoming weak because you are suddenly no longer in control? Are others aware that you are gradually sinking and incapable of doing things? Are they concerned that you are suffering from depression or burn-out? You ask yourself, who in the world can help you now? Your family doctor, your partner, somebody who understands what's going on with you!

In order to prepare, ask yourself the following questions:

- What can you do to experience personal happiness every week, perhaps even every day? What is fun for you? What brings you inner joy and satisfaction?
- What stress factors continuously flow into your life? Since too much stress is extremely debilitating on the body and mind, identify what you can and will now put to one side.
- With whom can you discuss your fears and worries? With whom can you discuss your inner feelings and insecurities?
- Find ways to serve. Serving others will change your perspective, as you see that not everything revolves around you! In the end, you will receive that which you give. Find ways to help others regularly. What might some of these suggestions be?

6. Addiction—the day you realize that something else controls your life. If today you realize that you depend on something external in your life, you are in seriously troubled waters. You might have thought yourself safe and incapable of falling into an addictive lifestyle, but regardless of whether your addiction is alcohol, drugs, a pathological relationship, pornography or gambling, you are in serious trouble. You are not really a free person. You are dependent on something. It doesn't matter how intelligent you are, how much money you have or how big your house is; you no longer have complete control over your life, perhaps no control; and so you had better get help now rather than later. (If it is not you who has the problem but someone who is close to you, this information is still relevant for you.)

It would be a big mistake to ignore this warning. The boardrooms, cockpits of large aircraft and high-achievers of our culture are affected as well as the poor homeless souls huddling in railway stations. Your life can also take a downward spiral and land in a place that is very foreign to where you are now.

In order to prepare, make an honest inventory of all the things you now need in order to feel good. Pay particular attention to alcohol, pills, nicotine, games and everything else that you "treat" yourself with—especially things that you don't want others to know about. Count the number of glasses, bottles, cigarettes, lottery tickets, casino visits, prescription pills and everything else that you consume.

This is your list—no one else will see what you have written. If you are not comfortable with what is on your list or if you are frightened by what you see, talk to your coach about it or get professional help.

7. Existential crisis—the day you lose the meaning of life. This seems to happen to all of us at some point in time. We ask ourselves: "What is this all about?" or "What is the meaning in this existence?" or "What is the purpose of life?" Perhaps you have the feeling that nothing really matters anymore. Maybe you do not really feel needed or of worth.

It slowly becomes apparent to you that you have not found any satisfactory answers to important questions for your children or grandchildren, that you can only answer them partially, or that you are no longer satisfied with your earlier solutions. If you are at this point, your life will certainly become difficult.

"He who has a 'why' to live for can bear almost any 'how'."
~ F. Nietzsche, Sprüche und Pfeile

Without your personal "why," you may be overpowered by even the smallest of challenges in life. When the day comes that this crisis appears, do you know where to take refuge?

In order to prepare, ask yourself these questions:

- What literature do you read for your personal wisdom and growth? Does it come from the Holy Scriptures, poets and philosophers? Invest time every day in studying wisdom literature. Many people before you have already gone that path successfully.
- Where do you want to be when you feel empty? Where do you refill your energy so that you can be reinvigorated and motivated in all areas of your life? Is it in church, the meditation group, in nature, with family or giving loving service to others?
- Is there anyone with whom you have "a score that you want to settle"? Is there an unspoken resentment or criticism? Whatever is still "open" in your life, you should work to clarify it, so you can say with a clear conscience and a clear heart: "I am at peace with myself and with others."
- What gave you the most power and clarity as a child and teenager? Can you imagine building on these old sources of power again today? What worked for you? How does your personal compass function?

GROW—This checklist will accelerate your growth in preparing for crises:

Checklist

1. Accept that crises are part of life. Make preparations for the time that you experience a loss; realize that fear is guiding you; become overstressed; become severely ill; control seems to leave you; you become addicted; or suffer an identity crisis.
2. Also prepare for common everyday situations such as: unemployment; debt; divorce; education; insurance; legal protection; business risk; and alternative courses of action. Work through these subjects for two weeks.

3. Make a detailed plan in which you answer all the questions asked. Use your learning diary.

Conclusion

LEARNING IS LIKE ROWING AGAINST THE CURRENT, WHEN YOU STOP, YOU DRIFT BACK.

Thomas: It was a beautiful summer evening in August in Munich. We met in Bogenhauser Hof in Munich for dinner. My conversation partner was a fellow entrepreneur Hans E. from Berlin, whom I respect for his personality and his work. He has managed to build a remarkably successful company within a few years and is now adviser and problem-solver in his department in the top division of the German economy.

For me Hans is a special mentor. In this conversation he gave me several tips for making my activities and projects more successful. Among other things, he showed me an exercise that I have since done every day. I now pass it to you. I am convinced that you will substantially increase your level of goal achievement and accelerate your progress to your destination. This exercise puts you on autopilot toward your goal.

Hans' Daily Exercise

"The human psyche needs a clear guide and a daily reflection of success," he explained. "The application is very simple: You need to apply it with discipline five minutes every day. That's what I have been doing for 11 years now, and it's incredible what has happened."

When he instructed me in the exercise, I said: "I will put it into action immediately!" I invite you to carry out this simple but powerful exercise with absolute consistency.

To start, you need a special notebook and pen. On the last page of the notebook **write your three most important professional and three major private goals**. Visualize the goals with a picture that you glue in. Every night, look at the last page, connecting in thought with the aim, and then go to the beginning of the notebook and write: *Every night, I typically write down about three points that have passed today in terms* *of progressing toward my goals.* This will be a success and knowledge journal on the way to your target goals.

Writing what went well causes many good things to happen. For example, this reinforces the idea that you are already on the way. You realize that doing three simple things every day brings you closer to your goals. By putting these things in writing, you compliment yourself—you express appreciation for your efforts, which has a reinforcing effect. It is a message to your subconscious mind: "You are successful today."

"Do the exercise," Hans said. "It will be self-perpetuating." These were his last words to me that evening in Munich—and that's what it has become: self-perpetuating.

What Might Derail You

There is a crucial factor for failure in life: *to spend time with things and people who oppose your goals or prevent you from reaching them*.

Focus on your main goals—your primary objectives. Do not waste unnecessary energy on secondary objectives—proceed forward with clarity and focus.

> *"Spend some time alone every day."*
> ~ *Dalai Lama*

Evening reflection. Remember and be thankful for what went well today: "Time spent with ourselves" lets us complete our day's work and daily experience with satisfaction.

Daily affirmation. You are now ready for continuous success in life. You now have the tools to create your opportunities and to use your strengths. Now go and continuously meet your goals. Trust yourself and your successes.

> *"In times of triumph too often the seeds*
> *are laid for a future defeat,*
> *as well as the seeds of a future victory can*
> *be sown even in times of defeat."*
> ~ *Daisako Ikeda*

Difficulties and crises are inevitable, and you will undoubtedly face larger obstacles on your way. These force us to increase our achievements—in perfect happiness no one will ultimately evolve. If you face your challenges, you can conquer them with force. Your inherent, and now strengthened energy sources, and your sharpened mind, will help you to achieve good. To be thrown back upon oneself, is to grow. Trust your personal inner wisdom.

Do not settle for a mediocre result. Please be and remain men and women of action. Please be not afraid to err in matters that life presents to you. It is better to make mistakes and to gain new experiences from them, than to accept the status quo, to not act at all, to be stagnant, to live in fear of making mistakes.

Justin: The joy of living with intent is found in the journey not the destination. As I strive to coach and live these principles, I have learned that people who really invest in mastering the first four principles of Live with Intent are the ones with the biggest, boldest and meaningful life plans. The power of Your Plan in principle five flows from principles one to four. Your plan then feeds all the remaining principles, which are designed to transform your plan into reality.

The speed at which your plan becomes reality is less relevant than the direction you are going and the joy you are feeling along the way. Be patient with yourself and enjoy the challenge of creating your future one day at a time. Live in the moment, seeing and doing the things that truly fulfill you.

Why Keep a Journal?

Thomas: I will never forget a special occasion with Justin in Salt Lake City, Utah. We were part of the European Team attending FranklinCovey's International Leadership Summit. Special sessions for CEOs were part of the program, and Justin pulled all the strings to get us in. The event was outstanding for me, and one detail still stands out today. It was announced that Michael Gorbatchev would speak at that Summit. Having grown up in the former West Germany, I had experienced the division of East and West Germany firsthand. So here he was, *Mr. Perestroika.* I still remember how excited I was when I was able to ask a question. I wanted to know how he prepared for the changes that he was the catalyst for. And I was so moved by what he said. He said that when he was going to university in Moscow, he had to take a long train ride every day. To pass the time, he carried around a small booklet, in which he used to take notes while traveling. He took detailed notes about his observations of how people were coping with life in the Soviet Union at the time. Later, when he was in the Kremlin and in charge of leading that vast country, he looked into that notebook—and those thoughts became the foundation of what we know by the name *Perestroika.*

So take the time—take notes. Keep a success journal, a learning diary. Whenever you reach your personal Kremlin, you will know where to look for your program!

Authentic Leadership

Before you know it you will be asked to lead others, not just yourself. The personal victory you will create by applying the twelve principles we covered together will set you up to become an authentic leader. Our dear friend Ken Shelton is an example of being authentic—in a world that has become increasingly unreliable. He taught us that...

1. Leadership is manifest in your love of vocation and avocation.
2. Authenticity is evident in every role and dimension of life.
3. Loyalty and fidelity are seen in daily duty to family, faith and profession.

We encourage you to identify authentic leaders that are an example for your life and draw lessons from their influence on you.

TIP

SEE

See your successes in your ***success journal.*** You can do so by applying the Hans' Daily Exercise as pointed out on previous pages. Daily in the evening reflect the three things that went well that day on the way to your goal.

DO

A. Document the results. Document the results of your learning achievements and insights when reading *Live with Intent*. Write down everything you have experienced in the past few weeks and months in your personal and professional life in your success journal. What were three key insights for you? What were the three most remarkable results that you achieved?

B. Teach others. The best way to keep the principles you've learned alive is to teach them to other people and help them as they put the teachings to use. This deepens and reinforces what you have already learned. Invite a friend and tell her or him about *Live with Intent*. Summarize your most important principle in a five-minute presentation.

GROW—Please tell us about your challenges and successes. We will rejoice with you about your successes and empathize with your challenges. If you always have this book in your life, you can achieve amazing things.

In our lives, these principles have enabled us to achieve many successes. Our desire is to share this content with you. Integrate your favorite exercises into your daily and weekly schedule. Also take a look from time to time at some of the "less loved ones." Maybe there is an exercise among the group that wants to "move up" and grow.

Try to perfect your mental powers and abilities. These techniques are like a second language that you have learned. It requires steady training to become and remain fluent; once you've mastered this new language, you'll be better able to navigate through successes and failures in life.

Good luck! Enjoy the steps towards your personal horizon!

ABOUT THE AUTHORS

Thomas Reichart and Justin Tomlinson met in Europe in 1998 where they worked together opening Continental Europe for Franklin Covey. Three years later they founded Reichart Effectiveness Consulting in Germany, and in 2008 Justin founded the ValueAdd group in Switzerland.

For over 20 years, **Thomas Reichart** has been a management trainer, executive coach and change management consultant. His repertoire includes the areas of personal effectiveness, managerial effectiveness, success methodology and performance psychology. He advises companies, service providers and teams on an international level. *Reichart Effectiveness Consulting* is known for its expertise in developing leadership skills within client organizations with a value-oriented and systemic approach. Thomas completed a BBA at GSBA Zurich, an MBA at Duke University in the United States and an MBA in consulting and systemic organizational development at the University of Augsburg.

Since age 10, Thomas has been a passionate flyer. He has been trained as a glider pilot in Bavaria; and then at the age of 17, while living in the United States, he passed the test to be a private pilot for gliders and motor engines. He has been trained for night flying, instrument flying, aerobatics and high-altitude flight. For many years, he flew old-timer airplanes (1938 to 1945) in air shows.

While still in school, Reichart ran a publishing house and a seminar company and was a regular coach for success methodology and performance psychology. He then worked as manager of an IBM-AS/400 publishing company and was a member of the board of a major German trade publisher. He was the founder and CEO of the first nationwide online food delivery services in Germany. He was also European CEO of the world's largest consulting firm in the field of leadership as well as being a Company Manager of a global American family concern.

He has spent several years living and working in the United States and England. He is a father of three children and now lives in southern Germany.

Justin Tomlinson is a professional facilitator advising boards and senior management on the people side of value creation and the elimination of *Fakework*. He contributed to *The Complete Business Process Handbook,* a comprehensive body of knowledge around Business Process Modeling and Business Process Management. The book was designed as a practical guide for practitioners, managers, executives and students.

Justin is also the author of *A Pattern for Living a Life that Matters*, the story of how he and his wife discovered their value-add. He is a master life coach for naming and claiming your value-add as you live life on your own terms. He has pioneered several innovative talent development solutions including BETTeRprogram.com and the Entrepreneur's Academy. His passion is helping individuals and organizations grow their value add.

Justin graduated from Brigham Young University with his BBA in Entrepreneurship. His family moved back to the USA in 2010 after living in Europe for 12 years. He travels back and forth between the USA and Europe monthly.

BIBLIOGRAPHY

General:

Simon, Fritz (2008): *Einführung in die Systemtheorie und Konstruktivismus*, Carl Auer Verlag

Doppler, K./C. Lauterburg (2002): *Change Management. Den Unternehmenswandel gestalten. Frankfurt,* New York: Campus. 10th edition

Königswieser, R./A. Exner (1999): *Systemische Intervention. Architekturen und Designs für Berater und Veränderungsmanager.* Stuttgart: Klett-Cotta

Kneer, G./A. Nassehi (1993): *Niklas Luhmanns Theorie sozialer Systeme. Eine Einführung.* Munich: Fink

Watzlawick, P. (Ed.)(1997): *Die erfundene Wirklichkeit. Wie wissen wir, was wir zu wissen glauben? Beiträge zum Konstruktivismus.* Munich: Piper

Tomaschek, N. (2003): *Systemisches Coaching. Ein zielorientierter Beratungsansatz.* Vienna: Facultas

Varga von Kibéd, Matthias/Insa Sparrer (2005): *Ganz im Gegenteil. Tetralemmaarbeit und andere Grundformen Systemischer Strukturaufstellungen—für Querdenker und solche die es noch werden wollen.* Heidelberg: Carl-Auer-Systeme, 5th edition

Mintzberg, Henry (2004): *Managers not MBAs. A Hard Look at the Soft Practice of Managing and Management Development,* Berrett- Koehler

Referring to chapters:

Introduction:

De Vega, Lope (1992): *Alle Bürger sind Soldaten*, see Michael Olmert: *The Smithsonian Book of Books*, Smithsonian Books, Washington

Carr, Nicolas (2010) *Wer bin ich, wenn ich online bin...und was macht mein Gehirn solange?*, Karl Blessing Verlag

Sprenger, Reinhard K. (2004): *Die Entscheidung liegt bei Dir*, Campus Verlag

Chapter 1:

Covey, Stephen M.R. (2006): *The Speed of Trust*, Free Press/ Simon & Schuster Tracy, Brian (2003): *Das Maximum Prinzip*, Campus Verlag

Allen, David (2001): *Getting Things Done*, Penguin Books

Christensen, Clayton M (2012): *How will you measure your life?*, HarperCollins Publishers

Maschmeyer, Carsten (2012): *Selfmade*, Ariston Verlag

Seiwert, Lothar (2011): *Ausgetickt*, Ariston Verlag

Real Business Cases

Bower, J. L., *Sam Palmisano's Transformation of IBM*, in: Harvard Business Review, 01/20/2012, https://hbr.

org/2012/01/sam-palmisanos-transformation, accessed on 10/16/2015

Harvard Business Manager, *Harvard-Gespräche. Topmanager im Interview: Was Sie von den Grossen lernen können*, in Edition 3/2015, accessed on 08/25/2015

Harvard Business Review, *Managing Investors*, in June 2014 Issue, https://hbr.org/2014/06/managing-investors, accessed on 10/18/2015

The Center for Global Enterprise, *Competing in the Global Era—Explore selected insights from Re-Think*, p. 16, http://thecge.net/slideshare/, accessed on 10/18/2015

Chapter 2:

Gawain, Shakti (1978): *CreativeVisualization*, Bantam

Real Business Cases

www.wikipedia.de, Skandinavisches Design, https://de.wikipedia.org/wiki/Skandinavisches_Design, accessed on 10/26/2015

www.cultofmac.com, 12 Of The Best Apple Print Ads Of All Time (Gallery), http://www.cultofmac.com/196454/12-of-the-best-apple-print-ads-of-all-time-gallery/, accessed on 10/27/2015

Chapter 3:

Tracy, Brian (2008): *Eat that frog*, Gabal Verlag

Tracy, Brian (2009): *Flight Plan*, Gabal Verlag

Drucker, Peter (1966), *The Effective Executive*, Harper Business Essentials

Covey, Stephen et al (1994): *First Things First*, Simon & Schuster

Allen, David (2008): *So kriege ich alles in den Griff*, Piper Verlag

Koch, Richard (1998): *Das 80/20 Prinzip*, Campus Verlag

Real Business Cases

Dorfs, J. (2007), *Die Herausforderer. 25 neue Weltkonzerne, mit denen wir rechnen müssen*, Hanser

Hansen M.T., Ibarra H., Peyer U., *The Best-Performing CEOs in the World*, in Harvard Business Review 01, 02 2013, https://hbr.org/2013/01/the-best-performing-ceos-in-the-world/, accessed on 10/26/2015

Bouw B., *Vale confirms CEO Agnelli's exit*, in The Globe and Mail, 04/01/2011, http://www.theglobeandmail.com/report-on-business/industry-news/energy-and-resources/vale-confirms-ceo-agnellis-exit/article574959/, accessed on 10/26/2015

Chapter 4:

Walther, George (2001): *Sag, was du meinst, und du bekommst, was du willst*, Econ Verlag

Braun, Susann Theresa (2012): *Achte auf das, was Du sagst*, vianova Verlag

Tomatis, Alfred A. (2000): Der Klang des Lebens, rororo Taschenbuch

Pasztor, Susann & Gens, Klaus-Dieter (2004): *Ich höre was, das du nicht sagst, gewaltfreie Kommunikation in Beziehungen*, Junfermann Verlag

Patterson, Kerry et al (2012): *Heikle Gespräche*, Linde Verlag

Real Business Cases

Spiegel Online, *Prozess in München: Ex-Deutsche-Bank-Chef Breuer verteidigt Kirch-Interview*, 07/28/2015, http://www. spiegel.de/wirtschaft/unternehmen/ex-deutsche-bank-chef-breuer-verteidigt-kirch-interview-a-1045644.html, accessed on 8/25/2015

www.abendblatt.de, *Wortlaut des Interviews mit Rolf Breuer zu Kirch*, http://www.abendblatt.de/wirtschaft/article107750348/ Wortlaut-des-Interviews-mit-Rolf-Breuer-zu-Kirch.html, accessed on 08/26/2015

Chapter 5:

Maaz, Hans-Joachim (2012): *Die narzistische Gesellschaft*, C.H. Beck

Röhr, Heinz-Peter (2005): *Narzissmus, das innere Gef*ängnis, dtv

Spiller, Jan (2008): *Astrologie und Seele*, MensSana Verlag

Real Business Cases

www.spiegel.de, *AWD-Gründer: Carsten Maschmeyer verlässt Swiss Life*, http://www.spiegel.de/wirtschaft/unternehmen/awd-gruender-carsten-maschmeyer-verlaesst-swiss-life-a-802373.html, 12/07/2011, accessed on 08/27/2015

Maier, A., *Gross, Mann, Sucht. Carsten Maschmeyer Der Selfmademilliardär gibt gern den smarten Superfinanzier. Ist er aber nicht*, in Manager Magazin 09/2015

Maschmeyer, C. (2012): *Selfmade. Erfolg reich leben*, 4th edition, Ariston

Chapter 6:

Constitution of the WHO, July 22, 1946, New York

Gross, Günter F. (1989): *Beruflich Profi, privat Amateur*, verlag moderne industrie, Landsberg

Covey, Stephen (1989): *7 habits of Highly Effective People*, Simon & Schuster, New York

Pink, Daniel H. (2009): *Drive, The surprising truth about what motivates us*, Riverhead Books

Dr. Bergner, Thomas M.H. (2005): *Lebensmuster erkennen und nutzen*, mvg Verlag

Dr. Bergner, Thomas M.H. (2007): *Burnout-Prävention*, Schattauer Verlag

Spitzer, Manfred (2012): *Digitale Demenz*, Droemer Verlag

Real Business Cases

Roddick, A. (2001): *Die Body Shop Story. Die Vision einer aussergewöhnlichen Unternehmerin*, Econ

www.thebodyshop.de, Unser Unternehmen, http://www.thebodyshop.de/about-us/aboutus_Company.aspx, accessed on 08/27/2015

www.statista.de, Einzelhandelsumsatz von The Body Shop weltweit in den Jahren 2010 bis 2014 (in Millionen Euro), http://de.statista.com/statistik/daten/studie/255799/umfrage/umsatz-von-the-body-shop/, accessed on 08/27/2015

www.thebodyshop.de, Werte, http://www.thebodyshop.de/werte/inhaltsstoff-marulaoel.aspx, accessed on 08/27/2015

Chapter 7:

Erb Kristine (2001): *Die Ordnungen des Erfolgs*, Kösel Verlag

Häusel, Hans-Georg (2003): *Think Limbic*, Haufe Verlag

Real Business Cases

Dörner S., Fuest B., Seibel K., *Das rätselhafte Firmengeflecht Rocket Internet*, 05/27/2015, in: www.welt.de, http://www.welt.de/wirtschaft/webwelt/article141524662/Das-raetselhafte-Firmengeflecht-Rocket-Internet.html, accessed on 09/09/2015

Mac R., *Germany's Samwer Brothers to become billionaires with Rocket Internet IPO*, 07/31/2014, in: www.forbes.com, http://www.forbes.com/sites/ryanmac/2014/07/31/samwer-brothers-billionaires-rocket-internet-ipo/2/, accessed on 09/09/2015

Koch B., *Thermomix-Boom beflügelt Vorwerk*, in Frankfurter Allgemeine Zeitung, 05/21/2015, http://www.faz.net/aktuell/wirtschaft/thermomix-boom-teurer-kuechengeraete-befluegelt-staubsauger-hersteller-vorwerk-13605125.html, accessed on 09/09/2015

www.vorwerk.de, Familienunternehmen mit Tradition, http://corporate.vorwerk.de/de/portraet/, accessed on 09/09/2015

Chapters 8 and 9:

Patterson, Kerry et al (2011): *Die Kunst, alles zu verändern*, Linde Verlag Wien

Ware, Bonnie (2013): *5 Dinge, die Sterbende am meisten bereuen*, arkana

Bauer, Joachim (2005): *Warum ich fühle, was Du fühlst*, Hofmann und Campe

Real Business Cases

www.autobild.de, *Neue Details zum Zukunfts-Benz*, http://
www.autobild.de/artikel/mercedes-f-015-vorstellung-5429797.
html, accessed on 08/27/2015

www.autobild.de, *Neue Augen für Mercedes*, 12/30/2014, http://
www.autobild.de/artikel/ces-2015-daimler-kooperiert-mit-
lg-5517649.html, accessed on 10/27/2015

cf. Page Larry on Google plus on 03/10/2015, https://plus.
google.com/+LarryPage/posts/THXDPTgTFcb, accessed on
08/27/2015

Page Larry on Google plus, accessed on 03/10/2015, https://
plus.google.com/+LarryPage/posts/THXDPTgTFcb, accessed
on 08/27/2015

Chapter 10:

Duhigg, Charles (2012): *The Power of Habit*, Random House

Leider, Richard J. and Shapiro,David A. (2002): *Lass endlich los
und lebe*, mvg Verlag

Sui, Choa Kuk (2010): *Energetischer Selbstschutz*, Ansata Verlag

Branden, Nathaniel (1995): *Die 6 Säulen des Selbstwertgefühls*,
Piper Verlag

Norwood, Robin (1985): *Wenn Frauen zu sehr lieben, die
heimliche Sucht, gebraucht zu werden*, rowohlt

Real Business Cases

Davies A., *How Elon Musk is revolutionizing two major industries at the same time*, http://www.businessinsider.com/how-elon-musk-overcomes-challenges-2013-3?IR=T, published on 03/13/2013, accessed on 08/31/2015

Guldner J., *Keine Pausen, kein Urlaub, kein Essen—nur Arbeit*, in www.zeit.de, http://www.zeit.de/wirtschaft/2015-05/tesla-elon-musk-spacex, published on 05/20/2015, accessed on 08/31/2015

Weddeling Britta, *Das Erfolgsgeheimnis von Elon Musk*, http://www.handelsblatt.com/unternehmen/management/biografie-des-tesla-chefs-das-erfolgsgeheimnis-von-elon-musk/11798852.html, published on 05/20/2015, accessed on 8/31/2015

Worall Simon, *Elon Musk, A man of impossible dreams, wants to colonize Mars*, in National Geographic, http://news.nationalgeographic.com/2015/06/150628-tesla-paypal-elon-musk-technology-steve-jobs-silicon-valley-electric-car-ngbooktalk/, published on 06/28/2015, accessed on 08/31/2015

www.tesla.de, Über Tesla, http://www.teslamotors.com/de_DE/about, accessed on 08/31/2015

www.teslamag.de, *Daimler Chef spricht im Interview über Tesla Motors und Elektrofahrzeuge*, http://teslamag.de/news/daimler-chef-interview-tesla-motors-2780, published on 03/30/2015, accessed on 08/31/2015

Chapter 11:

Beisser, Arnold R. (2009): *Wozu brauche ich Flügel*, Peter Hammer Verlag

Kreisman, Jerold J and Straus, Hal (2010): *Ich hasse dich—verlass mich nicht, die schwarz-weisse Welt der Borderline-Persönlichkeit*, Kösel Verlag

Real Business Cases

www.horstson.de, http://horstson.de/modemethode-karl-lagerfelds-kosmos-in-bonn/2015/03/, accessed on 08/31/2015

www.vogue.de, http://www.vogue.de/tags/l/karl-lagerfeld, accessed on 08/28/2015

Chapter 12:

Dr. McGraw, Phil (2008): *Real Life, Preparing for the 7 Most Challenging Days*, Free Press

Real Business Cases

Dorfs, J. (2007): *Die Herausforderer. 25 neue Weltkonzerne, mit denen wir rechnen müssen*, Hanser,

www.forbes.com, *India's 100 Richest People. 2014 Ranking*, http://www.forbes.com/india-billionaires/, accessed on 08/31/2015

www.wipro.com, Azim H. Premji, http://www.wipro.com/about-Wipro/Wipro-leadership-team/Azim-H-Premji/, accessed on 08/31/2015

www.wipro.com, http://www.wipro.com/about-wipro/, accessed on 08/31/2015